Charming Cheaters

Protect Yourself from the Sociopaths, Psychopaths, and Sexopaths in Your Life

Nicole Kelly, M.D.

JACC Publishing
6 Castlewood
Nashville, TN 37215

ISBN: 978-0-999-1861-5-2

Names, characters, places, and incidents have been changed to protect the identities of all persons. The information in this book is meant to increase awareness, NOT for diagnosis or medical advice. If you or someone you may know is a sociopath, psychopath, or sexopath, please seek professional help from a trained medical professional.

Kelly, Nicole.
    Charming Cheaters: Protect Yourself from the Sociopaths,
    Psychopaths, and Sexopaths in Your Life / Nicole Kelly, M.D.—
    1st Edition

Printed in the United States.

www.NicoleKellyMD.com

Dedicated to all those who truly care—
you know who you are.

Book Contents

Are you a
sociopath, psychopath,
or sexopath?
Hare
Psychopathy
Checklist-
Revised
90

<u>Chances are you know one...</u>

Chances are, you know a sociopath, psychopath, or sexopath. Using this book, you can spot these predators hiding in plain sight and protect yourself, your relationship, and your family.

Experts cannot agree on what to call people without a conscience. Really, it doesn't matter what you call them. If you have empathy, they are not like you. They can cause you and those you love harm if you do not recognize them as different. This is not about passing judgment. It is simply a reality that most of us do not understand. Recognition is the first step to taking our power back.

In order to make this confusing topic easier to understand, I have included a glossary at the end of this book. Before you begin, let me explain how I am using three important terms so we start on the same page.

<u>Psychopath</u>—people without a conscience or empathy at the far end of the spectrum. Although not universal, they can have lower I.Q.'s than sociopaths as well as increased aggression and lower impulse control. They make up 20% of the prison population. Imaging reveals brain abnormalities as well as altered neuro-connectivity.

<u>Sociopath</u>—people without a conscience or empathy who would probably not agree to be tested for an official diagnosis (such a label would be detrimental to their manipulative games) but do not quite make the cutoff to be full-blown psychopaths. Sociopaths have the genes to become people without conscience or empathy, but perhaps a better environment during development may be the reason they often have stronger impulse control enabling them to better wear a mask to fit into society.

In order to be less wordy, I will use the word "sociopath" to mean both "sociopath" and "psychopath" rather than writing "sociopath/psychopath" when both terms apply. The sociopathic/psychopathic spectrum will be called "The Sociopath Spectrum" for brevity.

<u>Sexopath</u>—sociopaths or psychopaths with a sex addiction. These sexual predators are responsible for much of the sexual misconduct by people in positions of power we see almost daily in the news. The Sexopath Spotting Tool is not only a way you can recognize sexopaths, but it can also give you the ability to identify sociopaths and psychopaths as well. Being a sociopath or psychopath is a requirement to be a true sexopath.

Introduction

Holding back tears, Brenda stares blankly at the computer screen. Ryan is dead. She repeats those words over and over in her head, but yet it seems impossible. How could this happen? Her son is gone. She had been so angry when he went out with his friends before cleaning his room as he promised. He was usually such a good boy. In a week, Ryan would have graduated from high school with a baseball scholarship to the college of his dreams. His whole future was before him until that terrible night when he was the passenger in a head-on collision that took his life. If only he hadn't gone. She should have made him stay to clean his room. Ryan is dead. The repetitive thoughts make her question her sanity. Brenda's world is crumbling all around her. Nothing is the same, yet she puts on a brave face and pretends to work.

You didn't know Ryan, but you have worked with Brenda for several years now. She is usually quick with a joke and has always had your back in meetings. It is terrible what happened to her son. You see her sitting at her desk about to cry. You place a hand on her shoulder and ask how she is. Brenda snaps out of her fog for a moment, looks up at you with pain in her eyes, and her grief stabs you through the heart. You can feel her pain. It tugs at your heartstrings and you even place your hand over your heart while you experience this physical sensation of empathy. For a moment, her pain is yours.

What is Empathy and Why You Should Care

Empathy is the ability to feel what another person feels. It is imagining yourself in someone else's shoes. Empathy requires the ability to understand what another person is feeling, followed by a sensation of connection to the other person that often is physical. It is a "tugging at your heartstrings." Empathy leads to caring for other people. It fosters the desire to do unto others as we would have done unto us, because we can imagine how harm we do to others would feel if they did the same to us. It generates much of our inner dialogues as we worry about how our loved ones are feeling and how we can help them.

EMPATHY = FEELING WHAT ANOTHER PERSON FEELS

I feel your pain

A TUGGING OF YOUR HEART STRINGS

For most of us, empathy is as automatic as breathing, but what if you couldn't feel empathy? Can you even imagine what that would be like? For most people, it is almost impossible to conceive of a life without empathy. The same is true for guilt and remorse. If we even think about hurting someone else, most of us have a little voice of conscience urging us to do what is right. We may not always do it, but the guilt that follows often makes us wish we had.

CONSCIENCE VS TEMPTATION

Conscience—The Angel on Your Shoulder

Conscience is something we empathetic people often take for granted. It is always with us. We can't give it the slip—or, if we are able to ignore it for a little while, it will catch up with us sooner or later with a huge helping of guilt. It is that inner feeling or voice that acts as a guide to the rightness or wrongness of our behavior. It is our moral sense. It is not simply understanding right from wrong—it is understanding right from wrong PLUS the urging from conscience to do what is right.

Although Sigmund Freud was way off the mark in his psychosexual stages of human development, his theory of the inner moral conflict affecting empathetic people when making decisions is quite useful in understanding the conscience. Do you remember the old cartoons where there is a devil on one shoulder and an angel on the other? This actually represents Freud's theory quite nicely.

The devil represents the Id which is the pleasure-seeking part of the mind. It ignores any possible consequences of a decision or action and, instead, focuses on the possible pleasure that can come from a behavior. It is impulsive and child-like in that it only considers what it wants—everything and everyone else be damned.

The Super-Ego or conscience is the angel who represents our ideals and aims for perfection. It considers how this behavior will affect others and what the potential consequences will be. It breaks things down into right or wrong and urges us to do what it considers to be right. If we ignore our conscience, it will hound us with guilt, shame, remorse, and regret.

To be clear: "conscience" is not the same thing as "conscious." "Conscience" is the little voice in your head urging you to do what you know is right. "Conscious" means awake and not "unconscious" or asleep/passed out. It is time that we wake up to our internal moral compasses. In other words, let's be conscious about our conscience.

LIFE WITHOUT CONSCIENCE

No Empathy, No Conscience— Big Problem

Sociopaths, psychopaths, and sexopaths * are not like the rest of us. Their brains are not wired to experience empathy or have a conscience. This makes them fundamentally different—even though they look like us. Their emotions are shallow, and they are missing the nagging conscience that urges the rest of us to follow society's rules. Sociopaths are all Id with no Super-Ego. They are missing the angel on their shoulder.

Without a conscience, sociopaths are spared much of the anxiety and worry that occupies the thoughts of most people. Sociopaths are left with a painful boredom that they ease by thrill-seeking behaviors including manipulating, lying, and charming those with empathy into doing things to benefit their personal interests including sexual gratification.

Much of what we experience as human beings is based on our ability to connect with other people. We are social creatures who need others in order to

> *In order to be less wordy, I will use "sociopath" to mean sociopath and psychopath. I will use "sexopath" when discussing a sociopath or psychopath with a sex addiction.

enjoy feelings such as love, joy, and connection. Most people see the path to happiness—and even enlightenment—through helping others. If we choose a purely selfish path, it may be fun for a bit, but after a while we will begin to feel empty, lonely, depressed, and life starts to seem pointless. It is through our connections with other people that life has meaning—our children, our parents, our friends, our coworkers, and even our pets add the spice of life most of us hold so dear.

Sociopaths don't care about anyone but themselves. They do not have deep connections with others as they have no empathy or conscience. If we see someone's fingers get slammed in a car door, we cringe and may even grab our hand as we feel a simulated pain at what we just witnessed. Imaging studies reveal our brains even respond as if our hand had been hurt as mirror neurons fire in response to what we saw. Sociopaths simply can't do that. Their brains don't work that way. They don't wince at seeing another person's pain. They may even enjoy it.

Interestingly, sociopaths are quite good at recognizing what other people are feeling—they simply don't care. Sociopaths can see a mother crying over the

Being a sociopath means I don't care if I drop one

loss of her child and realize that she must be upset which means society expects them to act in a compassionate manner. They can perform the part of empathy quite convincingly—acting is part of the mask sociopaths wear to blend into society—but they do not feel the mother's pain. There is no "tugging at the heartstrings" as there is no connection to another person like the rest of us feel. It isn't the case that they do not *want* to empathize—the connections in their brains are not set up to respond that way.

Sociopaths truly believe they are better without empathy and a conscience—it makes it simpler and easier to manipulate the rest of us. As a result of our empathetic nature, most of us spend much of our time worrying about others—*What do our loved ones need? What do they want? What are they thinking? Do they like me? What are they thinking about me? Have I done enough for them? Am I giving enough? etc.*

Sociopaths don't do that. This means they have a lot of extra time compared to the rest of us and are easily bored which can be quite painful for them. They have decreased fear and impulse control which often leads them into reckless activities that may be dangerous or even illegal. Addictions of all sorts ease the pain of boredom and sex addiction is not uncommon. Sociopaths see the world as a game, and we are the pawns to be manipulated for their personal benefit. To them, we are too wrapped up in our own empathy to even realize that there is a game—and that they are winning it.

Using deceptive charm and lies, sociopaths have conned their way into positions of power. They run our country, our companies, and our churches—yet most of us are completely unaware of their existence.

Checkmate!

It is estimated at least 1 in 25 people fall on The Sociopath Spectrum. That means that most of us interact with one every day and don't even know it! They are extremely difficult to recognize because they look like everyone else. You won't be able to recognize them at first sight, as it requires multiple encounters with careful observation to detect these amoral game players. Luckily, The Sexopath Spotting Tool is going to make recognition possible.

My Story - It Could Happen to Anyone

Before America was hit by the onslaught of stomach-churning stories of widespread sexual misconduct across all facets of life from business to entertainment to politics to sports—all the way to the Presidency—I was just your typical physician in Nashville, Tennessee who was busy seeing patients, taking care of my family, and trying to make it through each chaotic day like everyone else. That was until my world was turned upside down by a sociopath—and yes, she was a sexopath as well—who embezzled over $700,000 from my medical practice bringing my business to the brink of bankruptcy. While I was busy seeing patients, she happily took the burden of dealing with the economic side of my business. Only later did I learn that doctors and dentists—dedicated to helping and serving people—are particularly susceptible to this type of criminal activity. But, we are not alone. It is estimated that sociopaths' crime and deception costs American society over $2.3 trillion dollars annually—and no dollar amount can be placed on the emotional and psychological toll of these manipulative con artists.

If it can happen to me, it can happen to anyone. Even the most respected researchers in this field like Robert D. Hare, Ph.D. who know the in's and out's of this disorder can be fooled by these chameleons' charm and deception. If you don't know they exist, however, the battle is already lost. The first step in self-protection is recognition which is only possible if you are armed with the knowledge of their traits and characteristics. Let me use my story to begin the conversation.

Several years ago, I had a respectable medical practice with several employees including an intelligent, friendly, ever-so-helpful nurse. She was incredibly charming and fun to be around. We became friends.

At least, that's what I thought.

SOCIOPATHS COST AMERICA OVER $2.3 TRILLION ANNUALLY

SOCIOPATHS FEEL ENTITLED

I found this nurse's boldness quite admirable. Her optimism and invigorated spirit were intoxicating to be around. My life was more exciting because I knew her. When she told me she could do anything, she said it with such conviction, I believed her. In many ways, she was almost like those well-spoken preachers who roam the country where I live and convince people to empty their wallets with just a few choice words.

As we got to know each other at work, the nurse claimed the billing company we used was a total rip-off. When I looked at the numbers, she had a point. She claimed she could create better results at a much lower cost. When I hesitated, she insisted. She promised huge financial rewards if she did my billing. When I expressed my concerns, she had ready-made answers. I was so busy with the day-to-day demands of my medical practice, I finally allowed her to handle my billing. With that commitment, I gave her my full trust.

This new-found bond brought us closer together. As we began to spend time together outside of work, we became close enough to share details about our personal lives. She told me about her husband and her popular teenage years as I opened up about my love life and awkward childhood. It was great to have someone so close to me with such a different perspective.

Sociopaths Can Be Hypnotizing

When she told me she recently signed up for an online cheating website, at first, I was shocked. I knew she was more adventurous than I was, but this seemed a step too far. As she began to share the dirty details of her trysts with her new "puppies" (what she called the men who served her), I was transfixed by her sultry stories. They were hot, wild, and extremely titillating. In the face of her charm and outrageous attitude, I dismissed my red flags about her behavior. I have always believed that it is not my job to judge other people, so I gave her the benefit of the doubt and hoped she would come to her senses.

She never did. I suffered a devastating financial blow to my medical

Nashville Kitty
"Meow"

Age: 28 (Pisces)

Location: Nashville, Tennesse, United States

Height: 5'2" (157cm)

Weight: 105 lbs (48kg) - Fit

Languages Spoken: English

My limits are: Limits?! There are no such thing!

Status: Attached Female Seeking Attached Male

Gender: Female

Smoking Habits: Not Specified

practice as a result of her theft and discovered I was simply a pawn in her ever-changing game. The nurse was that special type of person who could sell ice to Eskimos. She could bring a tear to a glass eye. I had been manipulated and conned.

When her online cheating escapades began to spill-over and destroy everything in their path, I found my practice in financial ruin. She'd always told me the bloodsucking billing companies left so much on the table, it turned out she was the one who lapped it up. She stole hundreds of thousands of dollars and used it to finance her wild network of extra-marital affairs. She stole my money. She betrayed my trust. I was devastated by the whole experience, I felt a line had been crossed.

First, I did as any sane person would—I fired her. Then I gathered my case together and sued. My underestimation of her mastermind continued however, as she was already several steps ahead. During the lawsuit, the nurse made a fool of me. My lawyer warned me she would have spent any of the remaining money she stole before we made it to the end of the trial—which could take several years. Even with a winning settlement, she would simply declare bankruptcy. The banks would get their delinquent funds first, while I would be left with a hollow victory and a six-figure legal bill. As for her going to jail, with her manipulative skills, it was highly unlikely.

Having given up on the lawsuit, I decided to analyze what type of person could so successfully manipulate and control me. After revisiting multiple medical manuals and numerous recent research articles, I came to the frightening conclusion that the friendly, fun nurse was a conniving sociopathic sex addict—a sexopath.

NashvilleKitty Is Born - She's 1 in 25

Not to sugar coat anything, but my first book, *69 Shades of Nashville: Sociopathic Sex Southern Style*, began as a revenge novel. The real NashvilleKitty betrayed me, and I started writing as a form of therapy to figure out how I could have been so gullible as to be duped by a sexopath. The more I wrote, the more I realized I needed to warn others so if they encountered someone like the nurse, they needed to be exceedingly wary. As I wrote down her stories through the voice of NashvilleKitty, fictionalizing as necessary for legal reasons, I began to notice a pattern in her sexopathic demeanor and lack of meaningful connections with others. What started as a nightmare, resulted in the perfect character study for the ultimate anti-hero—and NashvilleKitty was born. She is someone everyone is going to love to hate.

Although I learned in medical school about Anti-Social Personality Disorder (ASPD)–often used interchangeably with psychopathy and sociopathy (although there is great debate about the semantics that we

will get into later)—I had always imagined the classic, violent psychopath with lettered tattoos on his fingers, a history of arson, abuse of children and animals, and often serving a prison sentence. The (mostly) non-violent sociopaths had not been stressed in school. The mental and behavioral patterns the nurse had demonstrated, however, fit this category with a dose of sex addiction attached. She was a sociopathic sex addict or sexopath with many of the following characteristics found in The Sexopath Spotting tool.

GLIMPSE BEHIND THE MASK

- **G**uiltless* - lack guilt, no remorse, no conscience
- **L**ies* - lie as easily as they breathe, pathological
- **I**nfidelity - multiple relationships using deception
- **M**anipulative* - life is a game, people are pawns
- **P**redatory stare* - unblinking, see people as prey
- **S**exopath love cycle - idealize, devalue, discard
- **E**mpathy lacking* - can't feel what others feel

- **B**reak the law* - think rules do not apply to them
- **E**gotistical* - narcissistic, feel entitled, glib
- **H**ollow emotions* - cold, callous, no fear/love/worry
- **I**rresponsible* - unreliable, parasitic lifestyle
- **N**ot me* - never their fault, blame others/circumstances
- **D**anger seekers* - hate boredom, want thrills

- **T**argeting next sexual target - always on the prowl
- **H**ead honcho* - use power to manipulate others
- **E**xpressional inconsistencies* - fake emotions, wear a mask

- **M**agnetism* - superficial charm, mirror back to fool
- **A**nger* - fits of illogical rage over trivial things
- **S**ex addiction - often about control/conquest
- **K**ill for power and control* - want to win at all costs

* True for sociopaths and psychopaths with or without sex addiction

The real and the fictional NashvilleKitty are both sociopathic sex addicts or sexopaths. The novel sought to take readers inside her mind to show her convoluted thought processes. Although modified into a fictional format with all identifying information changed, my ex-friend supplied enough stories of her many sexual conquests to paint the picture of the sexopathic psyche in a very entertaining manner. By channeling her voice, the reader is able to enter the mind of a sexopath. This is truly how she thinks.

When giving lectures, I often find that too many facts and not enough story put people to sleep. As over 65% of people are visual learners, I added over 300 drawings to the novel that reveal the hidden reality obscured by the first-person sexopathic narrative. For auditory learners, I found a local Nashville actor with the perfect Southern sweet voice that sounds incredibly innocent as she reads the manipulative NashvilleKitty words—even NashvilleKitty's voice is meant to deceive like the sexopath she is. Some people listen to the audio book while following along with the illustrated print version of the novel for the craziest read-along ever. I wanted to create something completely outside-the-box, something that does not fit within any one genre: psychological thriller, erotica, mystery, fictional memoir, dark comedy, educational, graphic novel. I wanted to educate in an entertaining format, to teach without the reader feeling taught. Education does not have to be boring. So many people have said the novel is unlike anything they have ever read before. It is a completely new literary genre: Education plus entertainment or Edutainment.

Education + Entertainment =
I hate to be bored

Be Careful —
You might learn something!

EDUTAINMENT

The more I wrote, the better I felt. What started as therapy turned into a mission to educate the public about a type of person who sees us as pawns to manipulate for personal gain. As I drafted the last few scenes and passages to my novel, multiple horrific stories appeared on the news. They shared two things in common with the book: the sex and the sociopath. Significantly, the major difference is that all these stories seemed to feature men as the perpetrators.

Why This Book, Why Now

When the #MeToo movement began in earnest, women came forward, one after another, to reveal their own experiences with sociopathic sex addicts. At that point, I realized the behavior I'd witnessed was far more widespread than I possibly could have imagined. It turned out what I had witnessed wasn't a rare incident.

My story was only unusual in that the perpetrator was a woman. As the news headlines continued to mount, the explanations and accusations built the case that this was a male-only problem. Yet, my experience had taught me that it was absolutely not a problem exclusive to men. One possible reason for the hidden double standard is perhaps men are reluctant to admit being conned by a woman. They don't like to think of women as being sexually driven or manipulative. Even in cases of the fictional "femme fatale," the woman's ultimate motivation is written as a search for economic or political power or for an ulterior mission such as being a spy.

HOW DOES A SPIDER GREET A FLY?

It's so nice to eat you!

Even so, we know some women will violate the sisterhood code by stealing men and destroying families without a trace of guilt or remorse. What makes them act that way? Why would a woman take what is not hers, and then casually discard her conquest after the emotional destruction is done? She, just like the accused men making headlines as #MeToo perpetrators, could be a sexopath like my fictional NashvilleKitty inspired by the very real nurse.

If this behavior isn't tied to gender, something bigger is at play. Maybe this is a separate condition, a human abnormality. Maybe it just doesn't have a name yet.

In other words, while it's true that the majority of sexopaths are men (there is a biological reason for this that we will explore), it is evident this isn't a gender-specific disorder. It's not a problem exclusive to male society. All people need to be made aware of this problem.

While reading yet another report about an unexpected and horrific sexual assault, I decided the novel wasn't enough. As the sheer volume of sexual misdeeds mounted and perpetrators from every corner of society were implicated in the misbehavior, explanations began popping up for why it was all happening. People blamed power. People blamed locker rooms. People blamed chauvinism and gender inequality.

While all of these factors might play a role, lost in the conversation was any medical condition to explain the phenomenon. Someone needed to step out and speak up—and I don't mean about another case of sexual misconduct. Someone needed to at least attempt to give victims the balm to heal and those vulnerable the tools to protect themselves. Someone needed to call the phenomenon what it was.

#MeToo IS THE SYMPTOM

Sexopaths are real!

Why Not Me?

The product of this inquiry is the book you're holding in your hands. It's by no means an attempt to be comprehensive. I conducted no experiments. I am not presenting thousands of pages of quantitative data. This is solely from the perspective of both a medical professional and a concerned citizen who believes that a little knowledge might save people from the dangers that I—and so many others, to a much more severe extent—have experienced.

#MeToo and Beyond

SEXOPATHY IS THE CAUSE

In medical school, I trained in psychiatry and did additional psychiatric rotations during fellowship. For the last few years I have investigated all I could find on this topic and even completed additional training to administer the PCL-R as a trained medical professional. I use my knowledge of psychiatry on a daily basis treating my patients and view mental health equally important to physical health when treating the whole patient. As a board-certified hospice geritrician, I deal with the frailest of the frail. I meet patients and families when they are at one of the most vulnerable times of their lives. It is definitely a job requiring a conscience and the capacity to feel empathy.

I realize some medical professionals may question my qualitative findings. At the same time, some casual readers may not want to believe these dangers exist. But I think there are many of you who feel deeply that something is horribly wrong with someone who is a part of your life—you just don't know what.

I'm here to suggest that the "what" you've worried about can be captured in an eight-letter word: sexopath.

This book is organized to be a brief primer on sociopathy, psychopathy, and sexopathy—a handbook, if you will—with function the primary goal. It is designed to be useful to readers. To that end, I've tried to be as brief as possible about technical and biological matters while keeping the book compartmentalized so readers can flip around to a section that most interests them for initial reading or even re-reading for a more thorough analysis.

This is a serious subject. What is contained in this book could even save your life or the life of someone you love. This book is meant to educate the public about a dangerous group of people hidden among us. However, as I mentioned before, education does not have to be boring. I am a firm believer that drawings and humor aid in the educational process. Laughter releases happy chemicals such as endorphins into the bloodstream which may increase the ability for the brain to retain information. Activating more parts of the brain may help people understand and recognize a sociopath in the future. My goal with this book is to educate in an entertaining format, so I am going to employ the new literary genre of Edutainment. If it is fun to read, you are more likely to finish it and remember it. The book is broken down into two parts.

In *Part I: What is Sexopathy?* I will define what a sociopath, psychopath, and sexopath are and help readers distinguish sexopathic behavior from that of usual sexual behavior. Empathetic people can behave sexopathically—however, only a sociopath or psychopath can be a true sexopath. In addition, I explain the motivations and goals behind many sociopathic and sexopathic decisions. Rounding out this more explanatory section will be an examination into the ability of sociopaths to hide in plain sight—a sensible segue to identifying sociopathic and sexopathic behavior and spotting them. Recognition is the first step to staying safe in a sexopathic world.

Part II: Staying Safe in a Sexopathic World centers on how to begin to deal with sociopathy and sexopathy in the real world. I will provide The Sexopath Spotting Tool to give readers a sense of what sorts of behavior and traits typically fall into the sexopath category. The tool is written for sexopath identification but can be used to recognize a sociopath or psychopath as well. Characteristics that apply to all three are clearly marked. With an understanding of these warning signs, readers can become aware of the bigger games at play by sociopaths and sexopaths and can learn how to participate in them—or just avoid them all together—without getting burned.

Speaking of getting burned, the goal of this book is not a witch hunt where readers go around with a clipboard and check people off as sexopaths, but rather to provide them with some tools to avoid the mental—and potentially physical—pain involved with being unprepared to deal with sociopathic and sexopathic behavior. With ever present danger, there is an urgency to teach recognition and enable protection of readers and their loved ones.

AWARENESS = YES

BURNING = NO

Call to Action - Let's Take the Power Back

This book is a call to action. Sociopaths, psychopaths, and sexopaths are hidden among us in positions of power without concern for the greater good, but they have a major Achielles' Heel—they can't tell the same lie to everyone. If we—the empathetic majority—communicate with each other to expose the lies, we can create a different world. If a postion requires truthfulness and empathy—a sociopath is NOT right for the job.

Sometimes even news as relentless and overwhelming as the events described by the #MeToo movement can seem fake and unreal until it arrives on your doorstep. Like a reality TV show gone wrong, people who thought this sort of thing could "never happen to me" are often more devastated and underprepared to deal with such horrors if they only imagine they occur to someone else.

Trust me, this is not some Hollywood creation. This is not a distant threat. With one out of every twenty-five people on The Sociopath Spectrum, this affects everyone. It's time we call sexopathy by its name and take our power back.

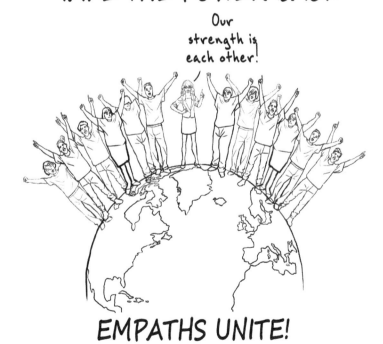

TAKE THE POWER BACK

Our strength is each other!

EMPATHS UNITE!

Part I: What is Sexopathy?

Chapter 1: If It Looks Like a Duck, Quacks Like a Duck - Treat It Like a Duck

WHAT DO YOU CALL A DUCK WHO STEALS?

Give me some bread!

A ROBBER DUCKY

Picture Kyle. He's a thirty-eight-year-old father. He lives with his wife and their two young girls, ages three and five. Their home is an upscale condo not far from his workplace. Since graduating college, Kyle has worked in the advertising industry. He's bright and personable. He's on a first name basis with the CEO and is particularly nice to the CEO's administrative assistant. To his superiors, he's the kind of guy who is very ambitious, confident, and takes frequent risks that seem to always turn out in his favor. He can charm the most resistant potential clients into coming aboard and has been rewarded handsomely with several major promotions in the span of his short career.

Upon first meeting, Kyle is a guy people want to be around. He's good-looking, with wavy amber hair and hazel eyes. He dresses in designer suits, drives a loaded Jaguar, and goes to the gym daily to maintain his muscular physique. He can converse easily about sports, politics, and the arts without making any enemies and is known for being a good listener. From the outside, everything about Kyle looks just about perfect.

But if you could be a ladybug on Kyle's lapel for a day, a far different picture would emerge.

Kyle kisses his wife, still asleep in their bed, when he leaves for work at 4:30 in the morning. She believes him when he tells her he likes to get in a few hours early before his colleagues arrive. Yet when Kyle drives away from their condo, he only travels two blocks before arriving at a parking garage at a nearby apartment building. He uses an unmarked key on his keychain to enter the building and always takes the stairs—he doesn't want to run into any other early risers—to the third floor where their daughters' babysitter lives. The babysitter won't head to Kyle's condo for a few hours, giving Kyle ample time to have steamy sex with her in bed and then again in the shower before they part ways.

SEXOPATHS,

I'm the best –
don't you
agree?!!

TOO GOOD TO BE TRUE

SEXOPATHS BELIEVE

I deserve a medal for all the love I give!

WHATEVER THEY WANT IS JUSTIFIED

Once he arrives at work two hours later, looking fresh as always, Kyle makes sure to engage in small conversation with the two new female interns who are both competing for his attention—and, ultimately, a job. It's just not the one Kyle has in mind. That's a fact already well known to one of the two young women, whom Kyle took with him one afternoon the week before to examine a potential conference site across town for an upcoming client meeting. The intern didn't realize the bathing suit she was asked to bring to test out the spa facilities at the newly remodeled hotel was optional until Kyle dropped his pants in front of her when they were alone. In the heat of the moment, she didn't exactly cave into his sexual suggestions, but neither did she turn him down. Now, he knew she was at least open to the possibility, and it was only a matter of time—and flirting with the other intern, her competition—before she submitted.

If Kyle is bored, for lunch he might arrange a "meeting" with an old client—a woman he knew in school who still holds out hope their fling might turn into something real—at her restaurant overlooking the golf course. The two have had an arrangement for years where they meet in the double-wide handicapped bathroom after ordering their food, to have a quickie right before the burgers arrive hot and steamy. He knows she could endanger his marriage if he doesn't regularly meet up with her, but he's also smart enough to realize meeting too often could have the same effect.

Afternoons and evenings Kyle likes to leave open—his wife still needs occasional sexual satisfaction but more than that, he likes to join his family for various community and school events. The more chances he has to meet women, the more potential fun he could have outside the office. Meanwhile, he frequently volunteers for long, monthly "business trips," which more often than not have him whisking off with a lucky flavor of the week for a lust-filled, company-paid sex fest.

By the time Kyle kisses his wife to sleep and closes his eyes at night, it seems inconceivable the amount of sex this pleasant fellow has had—or is intending to have soon—by the ease in which he sleeps. He doesn't toss and turn. He doesn't wake up. He sleeps as softly and quietly as an innocent child.

Do you know someone like Kyle?

Maybe you only recognize the first half of the description. You may know someone who checks all the boxes, seems to do everything right. They might be the type of person you enjoy counting among your friends.

Sociopaths' brains are wired differently

They might even inspire you. Perhaps, you think the second half just sounds too extreme to be true. You think, probably, someone could behave like that, but they wouldn't. Not in real life, anyway. There is too much at stake and something too morally distasteful for a guy like that to act that way.

Most people think that everyone thinks the same way they do, which is human nature. It's hard for us to conceive otherwise. And most of the time, for the empathetic majority, we're right. But that's just not the case when we're dealing with a sociopath or sexopath. Their brains are wired differently.

Kyle represents nothing less than one of the most relevant problems facing our society today.

We Are Not the Same

Not everyone thinks like you do. This statement is so incredibly obvious, yet it is almost impossible for most people to believe. After all, the way you think makes so much sense—to you anyway. It is human nature to assume that everyone thinks in the same way, and for the majority of people—those with empathy—they are right. However, for at least 1 in 25 people who fall on The Sociopath Spectrum, their minds function differently. There are people who lack empathy, guilt, remorse, and a conscience and these deficits make them think, make decisions, and interact with others in a way few of us are able to imagine—but this book is going to change that.

HOW EMPATHS SEE SOCIOPATHS

We are not all the same—including the experts. Research in the sociopathy/psychopathy discipline reveals experts who simply cannot agree on what to call people without empathy or a conscience. In fact, one psychopathy expert clued me into the fact that this field attracts many researchers on The Sociopath Spectrum—because narcissistic sociopaths absolutely love to study themselves! I guess that explains why they can't agree on anything and are often at each other's throats over how to define, diagnosis, and conduct research in this field. You would think their superficial charm would result in more research dollars—but that may be too much work.

SEXOPATHS LOVE GLORY

We will split it 50/50. You do the work -I'll take the credit

BUT HATE WORK

This lack of agreement between experts has led to much confusion and, in many ways, has limited effective research and education on this topic. Listed at the end of this book are many helpful resources where you can delve deeper into this debate, but my goal is to sum it up simply so anyone can understand. I am writing this for you—the empathetic majority—because most of you are not even aware people like this exist and that needs to change. By the end of this book, the light bulb is going to go off, and you are going to be forewarned. You will understand a type of person who has been, for all intents and purposes, invisible to you until now.

The Sociopath Spectrum: Manipulators to Monsters

These days there is a spectrum for everything. The spectrum model became most popular when describing The Autistic Spectrum. On The Autistic Spectrum, the range is based on physical and mental abilities while certain characteristics can be found at any level of the spectrum. I suggest we discuss the idea of people without a conscience or empathy using The Sociopath Spectrum. This is not a recognized spectrum by the research or medical community because this personality type is more complicated than a spectrum model can explain (also the research community prefers the terminology "psychopath" but more on that later). Dr. Robert Hare—or "Bob" as he prefers to be called (only FBI agents call him "Dr. Hare")—describes a dimensional model with multiple subtypes depending on how many traits an individual has in certain categories. Although it is very interesting, it is also very complicated, and it makes understanding this topic extremely difficult for the empathetic majority. Therefore, I am going to "big picture" it for you. I suggest you explore the Additional Resources section at the end of this book if you want to delve further into this topic, but my goal is to break it down simply so you "get it." The complexity of this topic is delaying the understanding that people without conscience exist and are all around you. Once everyone understands this fundamental point, then we can add back the many layers of this onion.

THE SOCIOPATH SPECTRUM

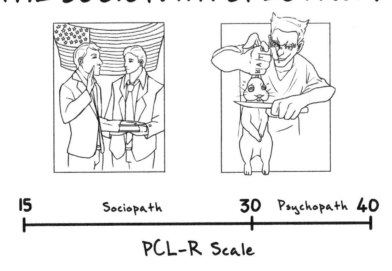

15   Sociopath   30   Psychopath 40

PCL-R Scale

The Sociopath Spectrum ranges from sociopath to psychopath with different levels of sexual deviancy along the scale. In order to differentiate the sociopath from the psychopath, some use points of intelligence, violent tendencies, impulse control, and incarceration to define the range. However, with any definition strategy, one can get lost in the details.

Distinguishing between the sociopath and psychopath based on aggressive tendencies, intelligence, and imprisonment is not accurate as sociopaths also can be violent, stupid, and go to jail. In order to give ourselves a way to visualize this complicated subject, let's consider it a spectrum—meaning that some people have less of these characteristics and traits at one end of the spectrum and others have a lot more at the other end. To even make it on The Sociopath Spectrum, the individual's brain function is fundamentally different from most of us. They do not think like we do. I suggest not getting caught up in figuring out specific labels—leave that to the researchers—because for you and me, the exact categorization really doesn't matter. In the end, determining where on The Sociopath Spectrum someone may be is not important. If someone is on the spectrum at all, we should carefully consider whether we want this individual in our lives.

Psychopaths:
Deception on Speed

Let's break it down. Robert D. Hare, Ph.D. (Bob) created what is considered the "gold standard" for the diagnosis of a psychopath using the Psychopathy Checklist-Revised (PLC-R) which takes six to eight hours to complete and must be administered by a trained professional—I recently completed the training taught by Dr. Reid Meloy and Bob himself. Bob's creation of the checklist was a huge step forward in this field, because it uses an extensive interview of the individual as well as collateral information from people who know the individual, police records, chart history, etc. The PCL-R accurately diagnoses psychopaths and has been repeatedly validated for several decades. Other methods to diagnosis this personality type use patient questionnaires. Although including thoughtful questions to reveal dishonesty, questionnaires are fundamentally problematic in this population known for pathological lying.

HOW DOES A CRAZY PERSON TRAVEL THROUGH THE WOODS?

They take the psychopath!

Per the PCL-R, the cut off for a true psychopath at the far end of the spectrum is 30 or greater out of a possible 40. The people who score this high on the checklist frequently have visible abnormalities on brain scans and their brains are even more abnormal when evaluating brain function—the areas felt to influence empathy and impulse control do not work like the rest of our brains. They are fundamentally different—and no pill or form of therapy has been discovered that can "fix" their brains. In fact, therapy often makes them worse as they use it to further hone their manipulative skills. The psychopaths glamorized by Hollywood such as Hannibal Lector, Freddy Krueger, and Alex from *A Clockwork Orange* would fall into this category.

Most of the research in this field has been on criminals or "unsuccessful psychopaths," and the estimated rate of true psychopaths in society at large is 1-2% (compared to around 20% in prison). There has been much debate among the experts about too much focus on the criminality or anti-social aspects of this disorder and that many people with these characteristic traits (especially those with higher intelligence or more money who are better able to escape getting caught and going to prison) are missed using current evaluation techniques. During training, it was recommended to use the PCL-R as a dimensional scale with greater than 30 meaning "Very High Psychopathy"—and lower scores representing "Mild to Moderate to High Psychopathy" which sounds an awful lot like a spectrum to me. An empathetic person scores a 5 or less, so someone who scores at least a 15 on the PCL-R is different from you and me.

This book will *not* enable you to diagnosis a psychopath—only the trained professionals can do that—but by understanding the characteristics and traits of the psychopath (and their "psychopath-lite" counterparts also called "successful psychopaths" or "sociopaths" or several other terms since the experts can't agree), then you will be better able to spot people without empathy and adjust your methods of interaction accordingly. Knowing that another person is operating in this world using different rules of morality than the rest of us will enable those with a conscience to better protect themselves from manipulation and betrayal.

Sociopaths: Psychopath-Lite

So, what about the "successful psychopaths" — who are not beating down doors to participate in the PCL-R or get their brains scanned? What about those people who don't quite make the cut off of 30? Normal people score less than 5 on PCL-R, so someone who scores a 15 has 3 times the number of psychopathic traits and characteristics than the rest of us. We are not the same.

In order to give us words to discuss these people who are so different from the rest of us, I suggest we use the word "sociopath" to represent those on The Sociopath Spectrum who do not quite meet the cutoff for psychopath. The researchers may not approve of the word "sociopath," but as a clinician, I think the word "psychopath" is confusing to the empathetic majority. Psychopaths are not "psycho" or "psychotic" which are common terms used in the community and lead to further misunderstanding.

For this reason (and to be less wordy), I am going to preferentially use the word "sociopath" to mean both "sociopath" and "psychopath" when both terms apply. The words we use should not hinder the awareness of people without conscience.

Sociopaths are the "psychopath-lite" (a clever term used by Dr. James Fallon) who have many psychopathic traits but either because of better brain function (perhaps they have better brain connectivity in the areas regulating impulse control so are better able to blend in with society) or maybe because of social factors (higher economic status, better nutrition, lack of childhood physical or verbal abuse, a different culture), they are less anti-social than their psychopathic cousins at the far end of the spectrum—but they are still radically different from the rest of us—the empathetic majority.

A SOCIOPATH

Some say that psychopaths are born that way (nature made them who they are) and sociopaths are made that way (environment made them who they are). This simply does not seem to be the case. When people are on The Sociopath Spectrum, clinical studies suggest they have a genetic predisposition to be the way they are. Environmental factors such as physical and verbal abuse and other factors may or may not activate more genes to express the disorder to a greater degree—but the person had to have the genetic predisposition to be on The Sociopath Spectrum in the first place. All abused children do not become sociopaths and many sociopaths had a perfectly wonderful childhood. It is simply more complicated—as most things involving the brain are.

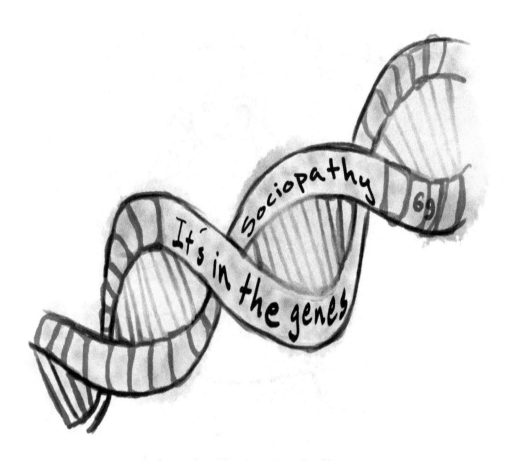

Some have argued that a huge environmental contribution for those with the genetic predisposition to be on The Sociopath Spectrum is the culture in which the sociopath lives. There are more people on The Sociopath Spectrum in Western society than in Eastern society. In the West, there is a higher value placed on the individual compared to Eastern society where the value of the group is often stressed. In Western society, being self-serving can lead to more success in business and politics, whereas stepping on the backs of others for personal gain is considered culturally insensitive in the East. Would someone with a genetic disposition for being on The Sociopath Spectrum have a higher likelihood of expressing those traits in a society where such characteristics are often valued? Some think so.

LIFETIME PREVALENCE RATE ASPD

United States	1.49 – 5.66% (no racial difference)
Taiwan	0.10 – 0.22%

In a small clinical study, psychopaths have been found to have identifiable abnormalities in brain scans with altered appearances in the frontal lobe and the hippocampus, whereas these structural brain changes were not seen in the sociopaths with much higher PCL-R scores than normal (over 3-4 times), but who didn't reach the 30 cutoff for the psychopath diagnosis. It is theorized that sociopaths have better brain connections (especially with regards to impulse control in delaying gratification—important in staying out of jail) than their psychopathic cousins.

WHERE DO HIPPOS GO TO COLLEGE?

HIPPOCAMPUS

Psychopaths appear to have absolutely no conscience or empathy, whereas sociopaths may have a little bit of optional empathy—that they can choose to ignore when it is inconvenient for them. They have the ability to switch the nagging conscience off while still having enough conscience to allow them to consider potential negative consequences of their actions that may not be in their self-interest. Before doing something reckless, sociopaths may consider the risk of getting caught and modify behaviors accordingly. Sociopaths may have twinges of guilt or remorse, but the signal isn't strong enough and doesn't last long enough to cause a change in behavior. Their wrongdoings do not keep them awake at night. They do not regret the harm they have caused others. It is as if their empathy and conscience are muted or dimmed—the connections in their brains do not respond in the same way as found in empathetic people who can't switch off empathy and conscience without exerting great mental energy. It really does not even qualify as the same empathy or conscience the rest of us experience. Their brain connections are faulty.

For the empathetic, the fear of a guilty conscience often will prevent our acting in a harmful way toward others. If we hurt someone, we feel bad because our empathy makes us experience some of the pain we caused. People on The Sociopath Spectrum simply don't do that. They do understand that their actions hurt someone else—they simply do not care. They do not have the fear of guilt or remorse to keep them from hurting others because the guilt trip never comes. Sociopaths simply do not have a conscience or empathy like we do.

Whether it is better impulse control, higher intelligence, lack of childhood trauma, increased socioeconomic status, different cultures, or better brain connectivity that makes the sociopath different than the psychopath, sociopaths tend to be better at wearing a convincing mask to fit into society and even can con their ways into positions of power and influence—often to the detriment of everyone else. Psychopaths on the far end of the spectrum tend to have a harder time blending in and will act impulsively and sometimes violently, frequently landing them in prison. Really, it is not necessary to get hung up on classifying people as sociopath versus psychopath. Both psychopaths and sociopaths know right from wrong and are responsible for their actions—they simply don't care. The distinction between sociopath and psychopath is not so important—the first step is to recognize that someone is on The Sociopath Spectrum and then to watch out!

SOCIOPATHS LACK
A CONSCIENCE OR EMPATHY

Most sociopaths and "successful psychopaths" are never officially diagnosed—such negative labels would hinder their ability to effectively manipulate the rest of us. Therefore, the exact number of people on The Sociopath Spectrum is unknown, but is estimated to be anywhere between 4% (1 in 25 people) but may be up to 10% (1in 10 people) by some reports. Those in power are even more likely to be on The Sociopath Spectrum.

Some claim that being on The Sociopath Spectrum—with loads of self-confidence, the courage to take risks, and the ability to persuade— gives them an advantage for getting ahead (especially in Western society), and if they follow a code or set of rules (such as those set up within religion), they can be productive members of society. Having a brain that functions differently does not make people evil—but it may predispose them to do evil things. That said, if a position requires truthfulness and an ability to feel empathy—a sociopath is NOT the best person for the job.

YOU KNOW A SOCIOPATH!

AT LEAST 1 IN 25 PEOPLE FALL ON THE SOCIOPATH SPECTRUM

Anti-Social Personality Disorder

Before I go much further, I want to clear up some very confusing word choices and overlap of definitions that has plagued this field of medicine. In the United States, the American Psychiatric Association—the largest professional psychiatric association in the world with over 37,000 members—publishes the Diagnostic and Statistical Manual of Mental Disorders (DSM), which is essentially the "Diagnostic Bible" for any medical professional dealing with mental health. The DSM was first published in 1952 with the most recent edition—the DSM-V—released in 2012. Because this book becomes the guide for everyone from lawmakers to pharmacists and physicians to researchers, it also receives its share of criticism (the DSM is used for the diagnoses submitted to insurance companies, and it is reported up to 70% of those involved in the most recent edition have a tie to pharmaceutical companies). Nonetheless, the DSM-V offers the diagnosis of Anti-Social Personality Disorder (ASPD) to cover the disorders of psychopathy and sociopathy.

The word "anti-social" is unfortunate as it is used colloquially to mean "asocial" such as a hermit or someone who doesn't like to be around other people—which absolutely is not the case for people with ASPD since people with ASPD need to be around people in order to manipulate them. It also turns out that much of the current diagnostic criteria focuses on criminality and a large percentage of criminals meet the criteria but are not true psychopaths when evaluated by the PCL-R. Sociopaths often do not meet the diagnostic criteria as presently written. Oddly, the DSM-V has an alternative section in the back that does hit the mark much better than the main criteria (and would really have helped to bring everyone to the same page), but, for some reason, it wasn't incorporated into the section actually used by the medical community (and the insurance companies who pay the medical community) at this time. To sum it up, ASPD is often used interchangeable with "psychopath" and "sociopath," but most experts in the field question its validity in its current form.

Psychopath, Sociopath, Anti-Social Personality Disorder, what do the differences all mean? The short answer is that the distinctions and nuances really don't matter. I am going to use the word "sociopath," but I hope this chapter was able to explain some of this confusing nomenclature. Whatever the name, the essence is the same–they have no conscience or empathy like the rest of us. Sociopaths are missing the ability to connect with another person on a soul-level.

THE DEVIL WANTS MY SOUL?

WHAT SOUL?

Sexopaths:
The Root of #MeToo

Sexopath. If you Google this word, there is no previous definition. Until this book, the word "sexopath" did not exist. The concept of sexopathy is my own creation—even if its existence in the real world is quite the contrary. After my experience, writing my novel on the subject, and the increasing visibility of a certain type of behavior in the public with the #MeToo Movement, I wanted to continue the conversation about the elephant in the room. To do that, I needed to coin a term.

I wanted to define the gap between those people who can suspend their empathy for sexual gratification and the majority of us who aspire to increase our empathy and deepen our connections. We simply need a word to describe these types of people. If someone doesn't have a term for a type of person with a type of behavior, they themselves will be unable to have an internal dialogue about how to handle that person. We need a word so that when someone meets a person who meets a certain set of criteria, they can realize that the person may be trouble and proceed carefully. Having a word enables us to identify potential danger.

That word is "Sexopath."

Sexopaths & Sex

A sexopath is a particularly dangerous type of sociopath or psychopath. It is bad enough when a sociopath or psychopath creates a hostile work environment, bullies family members, or uses a position of power for personal gain, but the sexopath goes for the heart where we are the most vulnerable.

The key to understanding sexopathy is to understand who sociopaths and psychopaths are. Because they are lacking a conscience, they are incapable of sex with empathy. Hypersexuality is a known characteristic of this personality type and sex addiction is not uncommon among sociopaths and psychopaths. Though sociopathy and sex addiction can exist on their own, it is in their coming together when sexopathic sparks fly. Like a nuclear test, you'd do well to be watching that combustion at a safe distance and with protection.

To be a true sexopath, first one must be on The Sociopath Spectrum, meaning being a sociopath or psychopath. Promiscuity is a known characteristic of those without empathy and addictions of all sorts are common—often sex being one of several addictions. However, you do not have to be a true sexopath on The Sociopath Spectrum to exhibit sexopathic behavior. Being under the influence of alcohol, drugs, or even out-of-control hormones can result in someone acting sexopathically—at least temporarily.

Sex Addiction

When it comes to sex-addiction in and of itself—a self-evident term many Americans are familiar with but may not be able to define—there is much disagreement. At present, the American Psychiatric Association does not recognize it as an actual disorder. It is not included in the DSM-V, although it was included when I was in medical school. The DSM-III called it *hypersexuality disorder*. Its removal was the cause of the great, never-ending debate on what is considered to be sexually "normal." Perhaps the biggest confusion comes in the case of cheating, where only those who are caught seem to have a "disorder," whereas if they'd gotten away scot-free, they wouldn't be part of the research in the first place.

The debate about sex-addiction gets muddied because of societal judgment, cultural norms, and resistance to label anyone's sexual preferences as "deviant." What we can conclude is that inherent in any addiction is the desire to get the "high" regardless of potential negative consequences and functional impairment. Many sex-addicts have over one hundred partners. Some even fail to orgasm. For many, it is more about the conquest and control rather than the physical release. There is often a persistent craving for sexual contact resulting in neglecting obligations in the pursuit of sex. Often there is increasing irritability when unable to engage in sexual activity. It frequently causes problems in multiple areas of life including home, work, and in the community. Sexopaths and, in general, all sex addicts are repeatedly scheming on how to get their next sexual fix.

The Biology in Brief

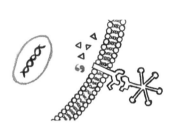

If sexopathy exists at the convergence of sociopathy and sex addiction, that means the features of someone with the disorder are somewhat difficult to see from the outside. Looking inside at what's going on behind the scenes—on a physiological level—can help us better understand why sexopaths exist in the first place. This will be helpful to us when we encounter sexopaths in our own lives.

Genetics

All of the usual debates apply when it comes to sociopathy and science. There is the nature versus nurture debate—how much of sociopathic behavior is learned and how much of it is inherited. Are sociopaths born that way or did circumstances create them? As always seems to be the case in medicine, the answer is both—in medical school, "All of the above" was frequently the right answer on multiple choice tests. There is a genetic predisposition for this personality type which can be more fully expressed under the wrong circumstances.

In studies done with sets of twins, it was found that identical twins who came from the same egg and have the same genetic material at birth are more likely to both be on The Sociopath Spectrum than fraternal twins who came from two different eggs and have different genes. This means something in the genes is related to expression of this personality type. They were born with the predisposition to become sociopaths. However, environmental factors may determine how fully the disorder is expressed. James Fallon, Ph.D. proposes if someone with the genes to become a sociopath has an abusive childhood, that person may or may not be more likely to be on the psychopathic end of the spectrum compared to someone who was not abused. Some studies with early intervention while brain connectivity is still developing in young children who are already displaying characteristics of this personality type have been promising.

However, growing up in Western society where many sociopathic traits are considered helpful to achieving success may hinder interventions in the young predisposed to sociopathy from working.

SOCIOPATHY IS GENETIC

ADDICTION IS GENETIC

Sex addiction has a genetic component as well. Animal studies show a gene called D4 linked to dopamine can influence sexual drive and arousal. Addictions in general are known to run in families with children of addicts being up to eight times more likely to develop addictions. Regardless of the type of addiction, it appears to work in a similar way in the brain. If you are in the 10% - 15% of people with the genetic predisposition to become addicted, your drug of choice—alcohol, drugs, sex, gambling, internet— may change, but your tendency for addiction won't (this also means if you are in the 85% - 90% of people who are not prone to addiction, you will not all of a sudden develop an addiction in your final days on hospice—so many people suffer at the end of life because of an unwarranted fear of addiction). Interestingly, the personality traits of impulsivity and risk-taking (quite high in sociopaths) contribute to the predisposition for addiction.

Mirror Neurons

When we try to discover where sociopaths come from, we have to start with the brain. The supercomputer of our bodies, the brain is multi-factorial. Without getting into the nitty-gritty, our brains contain mirror neurons which are observed in humans as well as in the animal kingdom. Essentially, they fire off in connection with things we do and things we see done by others. When we skin our knee, our mirror neurons fire off in a similar way as when we see other people skin their knee. As a consequence, these mirror neurons become essential to experience empathy.

Sociopathic brains do have firing of mirror neurons, but the emotional response is blunted. It had been theorized that those on The Sociopath Spectrum would have decreased firing of mirror neurons, but what was found surprised everyone. It seems that they do have the ability to *recognize* what another person is experiencing, but the empathy and emotional response to the recognition simply doesn't happen. They understand what someone else is feeling—they just don't care.

It turns out that people on The Sociopath Spectrum may even be *better* at recognizing emotions in others, but they do not *feel* the same emotion as the rest of us. Ted Bundy famously said that he could spot a "good victim" just by the way she walked. One interesting study by Angela Book, Ph.D. tested this theory as she showed a group of psychopaths different women walking down a corridor. Half of the women had a history of past trauma and, without fail, the psychopaths were able to pick out the ones who were the most vulnerable simply by how they walked. They were experts at selecting susceptible victims. It is theorized that this improved ability to recognize other people's feelings—while not feeling them themselves—makes it even easier for them to manipulate us.

PET Scans

There is ample clinical evidence that sociopaths' brains function differently. Positron Emission Tomography (PET scans) have shown decreased activity in both the temporal and frontal lobes of the brain needed for empathy and impulse control—especially for people on the psychopathic end of The Sociopath Spectrum. In some imaging studies, psychopaths have abnormal appearing brain structures that are even more

obviously different from empathetic brains when examining how the psychopaths' brains function. It appears faulty brain connections may be to blame which may explain why a sociopath can *recognize* others' feelings but is not able to complete the next step of *feeling* what others feel.

Damage to the brain can turn an empathetic person into a sociopath. For example, soldiers with frontal lobe injuries often will exhibit sociopathic behavior when they returned to civilian life. These soldiers were upstanding citizens prior to injury to the frontal lobe part of their brains, but after damage in these areas, the soldiers began to behave sociopathically—with no conscience, empathy, guilt, remorse, and often with reckless sexual aggression and multiple addictions.

People on the more sociopathic side of The Sociopath Spectrum have not been studied as thoroughly as much of the research has been done on the more psychopathic prison population who are happy to participate in research to lessen their boredom while incarcerated. Most sociopaths (not all, because sociopaths do commit crimes and sometimes get caught) are not in jail and are not volunteering for research studies that could potentially jeopardize their ability to get ahead. Additional research would certainly be helpful in sorting out the differences between the two ends of The Sociopath Spectrum.

Functional MRI - Words Without Emotion

In fMRI studies (Functional magnetic resonance imaging–where brain activity is measured by blood flow in response to stimuli), individuals on The Sociopath Spectrum do not react to words in the same way as the rest of us. They are unable to *feel* the emotion associated with certain words. For example, empathetic people will react quicker and have emotional areas of the brain respond to words with an emotional undertone such as "rape" or "cancer" compared to words like "paper" or "curtain" while those on The Sociopath Spectrum react at the same rate to all words and there is no emotional response. They can say the words "I love you" but the underlying emotion is no more than if they had said "I would like cream in my coffee." Researchers Johns and Quay described the phenomenon as sociopaths understand "the 'words' of emotion, but not the 'music'."

SOCIOPATHS REACT TO WORDS DIFFERENTLY

This again is pointing to possible brain connection issues in addition to structural brain abnormalities. It is possible that during the development of the brain before birth as well as during infancy and childhood that the emotional centers were not properly connected to other parts of the brain leaving the sociopath with a blunted emotional response. We—the empathetic majority—cannot imagine it because our brains don't work that way. Our empathetic response is automatic. Our brains are simply wired to respond with a conscience as we undergo our inner moral debate about what is right or wrong about our next decision. It has always been this way. Our brains are stretched to imagine such a different way of thinking, because we have never experienced it.

The same is true in reverse. Sociopaths don't realize their brains have muted emotional response because they have never experienced anything different. They don't understand what all our fuss is about as we struggle with deciding our next course of action while considering the consequences and morality of the situation. Sociopaths don't have empathy or a conscience interfering with their decisions. They just do what they want and don't worry about it.

By living in society, sociopaths have learned that empathetic people value empathy and conscience, and sociopaths are able to act as if they also value these qualities, but, inwardly, they see our empathetic nature as a weakness they can manipulate. Perhaps because they realize on some level that they are incapable of experiencing emotions as deeply as we do, sociopaths will target the most vulnerable as victims. In sociopaths' minds, the most empathetic people remind them of what they lack and deserve to be punished. Sociopaths use our emotions against us. However, despite their envy, we should embrace our empathy and conscience as these qualities allow us to develop deep connections, including love, with other people.

The Warrior Gene
(Perhaps Why More Men are Sociopaths than Women)

There are longitudinal studies and papers that delve into the possibility of a "warrior gene" across history. Although not the whole picture because multiple genes are involved, the warrior gene may be one of the genes that contributes to the creation of a sociopath. The gene is more often found in men than women because it lives on the X chromosome. Women have two X chromosomes, so if the warrior gene is on one of their X chromosomes, they still have a backup X chromosome to prevent the warrior gene from being fully expressed. Women would need to inherit the warrior gene from both their mother and father in order for it to be fully expressed. Men have only one X chromosome, so if the warrior gene is on it, then it will be expressed. Men do not have a backup, so they are more likely to express the warrior gene if they inherit it. This may explain why there are more male sociopaths than female. Again, it is not the whole story, and the genetics are not as simple as what we learned in high school biology, but this may be one piece of the puzzle. Both male and female sociopaths are often found to have higher levels of testosterone which may also be a contributing factor.

It is thought that the warrior gene served a purpose long ago, because it programs these individuals to protect the tribe at all costs. They have decreased fear of harm or death and will perform heroic deeds in order to protect their tribe. This can manifest in violent behavior, however, that may have been more beneficial in a tribal setting but can be legally burdensome in today's world.

THE WARRIOR GENE

MORE COMMON IN MEN

The Pleasure Center & Neurotransmitters

Core evidence found in substance abuse studies, which focus on the set of brain structures colloquially known as The Pleasure Center—including the amygdala (which helps to regulate emotions as well as many other roles) and the nucleus accumbens (contributes in the flow of dopamine)—have also been applied to other addictions, including sexual addiction. Essentially, the more physically dependent someone becomes on sex, the more the wiring in the pleasure center is altered, creating lasting chemical changes that affect behavior.

Although by no means absolute—rarely is science so cut and dry—these findings are notable in that they back up scientifically what many of us have seen in our social lives (and of course in the news headlines) about sexopathy.

My Pleasure
Center
is activated!

Getting to Know the Sexopath - Hopefully, From Afar

By finally providing this rampant behavior a name, it's possible to offer some clarity from which those of us on the outside of these disorders can hope to cope. In that spirit, here are the definitions of sexopathy:

A sexopath: a sociopath or psychopath with a sex addiction.

Sexopathic behavior: sex or sexual behavior without empathy—can be by a true sexopath but also can be done by someone with a conscience temporarily "on hold."

Sexopathic Behavior =
_____
Sex/behavior without empathy
(By true sexopath or by empath
with conscience "on hold.")

Sexopath = a sociopath
_____
or psychopath with a
sex addiction. Sex is
always without empathy
because they are unable
to experience empathy.

In other words, there are true sexopaths who are sociopaths or psychopaths on The Sociopath Spectrum with no conscience, but there are empathetic people who exhibit sexopathic behavior in some instances. An empathetic person can behave sexopathically at times depending on the circumstances, but the difference is found in whether the empathetic person ever feels empathy or guilt. Sexopaths never do. The intent and the aftermath of true sexopaths' sexual escapades are different from the empathetic person behaving sexopathically momentarily. We will delve into this interesting point further in the next chapter.

For the sake of the brief overview of sexopathy in this book, we will steer clear of the many rabbit holes we could go down in our discussion of the topic. Instead, a rudimentary understanding of the true sexopath can be achieved through an understanding of these three main ingredients about the sociopaths and psychopaths on The Sociopath Spectrum:

1. A lack of sexual empathy.
2. The desire to manipulate others as if life were a game.
3. The ability to avoid detection by crafting and using a mask.

These three key characteristics of sexopathy will serve as the guiding topics of the following three chapters in Part I before we go into how it all manifests itself in the real world in the second half of the book.

Chapter 2: Sexopathic Sex: All Sex - No Empathy

In a world where a woman is asked to do it all, Allie is exceeding expectations. She's a mother to a middle-school-aged daughter, a wife to a husband who struggles with depression, and a daughter to a set of divorced, aging parents who are both experiencing medical problems. On top of that, she's a lay minister at her church and hosts weekly prayer groups at her home for women of all ages. For all of these people, Allie is a rock.

She's also the breadwinner in the family. She pays for her mother's chemotherapy and her father's expensive blood pressure medication. Her daughter requires special attention at her pricey private school, and Allie takes on extra projects to keep the family out of debt. Her husband, who's been out of work for several years, does his best to keep his spending at a minimum but his cases of whiskey and cigarettes add up.

Allie's aware of the people who depend on her. She takes her responsibility toward them seriously. In fact, that's part of the reason she took a job at a product-testing company. The pay bump was significant and even though her new gig required a lot of travel, and her being away from the very people she was doing it all for, she took it knowing it will help everyone in the long run.

I love my family and will do anything for them.

It was about a year into the new job when she has her first one-night stand on the road. She finds the guy at a hotel bar. They go back to her room. They use protection, but it feels as free as she's felt in ages—and she actually has an orgasm, something she's felt like she's never had. It's the first sex she's had since her daughter was born. In the morning he's gone. End of story.

EMPATHS STRUGGLE

Pack Your Bags For Your Guilt Trip!

That was fun! Let's Do it again!

WITH MORAL CONFLICT

She comes home later that day and feels rotten. She even considers admitting it to her husband, but when she tries to bring it up after dinner, it's clear he's gotten more drunk than usual with the wine from the meal. Allie was so worried about the impending confession she hadn't noticed him open the second bottle, which she finds in the trash the next morning when she's leaving for work. She's still determined to tell her husband about what happened, but that night is the prayer group, and it lasts longer than usual. Her husband's asleep when Allie gets into bed that night.

Things keep getting in the way that week—a doctor's appointment for her mother, her father's birthday, and her daughter's school play. By the time she hits the road again, she's given up hope on telling her husband. She decides she will keep it a secret. It only happened once.

Except, on the next trip, Allie does it again. This time, when she notices a new guy at the hotel bar, she slides her wedding ring off her finger. By the time he approaches her, she's already decided to sleep with him and never, for an instant, refers to her being married or any details about her personal life.

Sleeping with men like this on the road becomes her new normal. She begins to look forward to it. On trips where the hotel bar is empty, she gets frustrated and is forced to pleasure herself alone in the hotel room.

On one trip, Allie spots an unbelievably attractive man. She decides she has to have him, slips her ring off her finger and approaches. It's clear he's emotionally vulnerable. He sips his drink and talks to her not unlike her depressed husband. Through the course of their conversation, she learns he's recently been dumped by his fiancé a few weeks before his wedding. For Allie, questions of right and wrong at this point go out the window. She just wants to get him into bed, even if it means she needs to lift his spirits and lie through her teeth about not being married to do it. It's clear he's desperate for love and affection, and she's willing to deceive him in order to get what she wants.

It works. They have sex—and not just once. They do it again in the shower in the morning and that afternoon between their separate meetings. It turns out he's in a related industry. They run into each other at a trip the next month and do it all again. Pretty soon, they are scheduling to meet up together for these sexcapades. After a year of their affair, he's like a completely different person: he's happy with a renewed sense of confidence. He tells her she's the shining light of his life and pries for her to reveal more about her personal life.

Allie half-lies to him, explaining that she lives with her terminally ill parents back home and that their hearts would break if they knew she was sleeping with a man before marriage. Of course, this is mostly true. Allie was even a virgin when she married her husband, but she allows herself to bend the truth, just this once, so she can continue to enjoy the experience she knows won't last forever.

She can tell that he really likes her. Maybe, she decides after the two had been sleeping together for a year, he even loves her. When she really stops and thinks about it—which she does from time to time, often on the plane when she is looking down at the patches of earth passing by below her—she is aware that she will walk away from him and his heart will be broken. She is willing to hurt him in order to have that physical release, that break from all the pressure, whenever she is out of town for business.

They continue to arrange their clandestine meetings at hotels across the country. She tells herself at some point in her life, she will probably mature out of this. Maybe when her daughter is older, and Allie can see more clearly how her actions have consequences. Maybe when those stakes are higher, she'll be able to stop. Maybe, she hopes.

Can you empathize will Allie? Or do you think her behavior is unforgivable?

Whatever you think of her and her situation, it's clear she has a conscience and experiences guilt and remorse about what she is doing. True sexopathic men and women don't have a conscience about this sort of behavior—not once, not ever. Allie isn't a sexopath, but like a murder suspect who pleas temporary insanity as a defense, she's acting temporarily sexopathically.

FOR THE EMPATH

I cannot be silenced!

Just ignore her. I always do

CONSCIENCE CAN BE IGNORED
BUT NEVER SILENCED

The Empathetic Person - Able to Love

To better understand a societal abnormality, it's vital that we define the sexopath's empathetic opposite. In my novel, *69 Shades of Nashville: Sociopathic Sex Southern Style*, the protagonist NashvilleKitty often refers to those who are not super-powered sexopaths like herself by calling them "neurotypicals." She uses this term because it puts her in her desired position of privilege compared with the majority of the population. The word *typical*, as found in the sample phrase "that's so typical of X person," is often used to describe something obvious and predictable (and usually undesirable). In NashvilleKitty's case, its function is to insult and disarm anyone she comes across in advance. Though this nomenclature is useful on the one hand, as it does help distinguish between those with sexopathic tendencies and those without them, it doesn't fully explain what a "non-sexopath" is. To make this distinction clearer—and to avoid using the rationale of a self-proclaimed fictional sexopath—we need to investigate our understanding of "everyone else" who falls outside The Sociopath Spectrum.

An empathetic person is someone who is capable—and often exhibits—empathy before, during, and after sex. Without getting too religious about it, often empathetic people acknowledge that the person they have sex with has a soul just like they do. They don't have to love them. They don't even have to like them—they might even dislike them. But they do not discount their humanity; they recognize their soul. An atheist might object to the concept of a soul yet can still have empathetic sex with an emotional connection to another person as a sexopath never could.

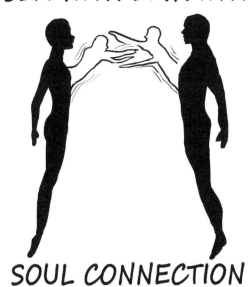

SEX WITH EMPATHY

SOUL CONNECTION

As explained in the first chapter, part of the reason none of these concepts appear in the DSM-V or other medical journals is because of how slippery a slope it is to attempt to isolate what can be defined as "normal" sexual behavior. Sex, in all its forms, is an animalistic act—a biological and evolutionary imperative that often can appear different shades of brutal and beautiful, or both at the same time. That's all before you begin to consider all the religious and cultural restrictions about certain kinds of sex.

Irregular Sex:
One Size Doesn't Fit All

The question, "What are you into?" when it comes to sex, will inevitably elicit different answers from different people. There are those with relatively tame fetishes: feet and ear nibbling, for example. On the other hand, there are people with more extreme sexual interests: feces and being choked. Whether an individual considers any behavior *irregular* or *unorthodox* or just plain *wrong*, will depend on whom you ask.

Since the dawn of humanity—and especially since the invention of the written word—guidelines for sexual do's and dont's have been drafted, disseminated, and revised according to the cultural climate of the time. One action a group of people might decide is acceptable or desirable in one part of the world at one particular time could be considered savage or inhumane elsewhere, at another time. That sex is inexorably linked with spirituality only complicates matters.

Human sexuality is often described as a line. Colloquially, any deviation from what's considered "normal" in a given place at a given time, is referred to as kinkiness. If you have some unconventional sexual interest, you have a *kink* or a bend in the line of sexuality.

Tantric sex and BDSM are two such examples of *kinkiness*. If we consider any sexuality as a spectrum between animalistic and spiritual poles, all sexual actions (including behavior that could be considered *kinky*) could be plotted on these poles. Tantric sex and BDSM describe two somewhat opposing *bends* in sexual behavior—no pun intended—with the former being closer to the spiritual side and the latter aligning more toward the animalistic pole.

For most Westerners, when we refer to Tantric sex we are talking about an idea of sacred sexuality that's often based on Indian Tantric practices. Though we won't get into the Sanskrit and religious underpinning of the Tantra, for our purposes tantric sex, like yoga, often involves participants contorting their bodies into positions most Westerners might be unaccustomed to, for prolonged periods of time in order to heighten a sexual experience. The goal aligns somewhat with sex as a vessel or vehicle to transcend the physical world and arrive on a new spiritual plane. Some people—both practitioners and opponents of Tantric sex—refer to it as a cult of ecstasy, where one's peak sexual pleasure is paired with their spiritual participation.

BDSM (a catch-all term built out of a combination of abbreviations for Bondage & Discipline, Domination & Submission, Sadism & Masochism) sits at a somewhat opposite end of the soothing-kind of spiritual sex offered by Tantra. BDSM is an umbrella term with dozens of other umbrella terms and communities underneath it. Much of the behavior centers on role-playing, where two people are put on opposite ends of a power dynamic and then act out towards sexual ends. The communities can include those with an interest in body modification, animalism, cross-dressing, and various fetishes for material (like rubber or metal) or instruments (like whips, chains, blindfolds, handcuffs, collars, and clamps). Though to outsiders these sorts of activities can appear violent or inhumane, these communities

Ready for
Enter-pain-ment?

often emphasize that behavior takes place between consenting adults who believe they have a right to do what they please with their bodies. There are other safety measures in place to prevent the behavior from hurting participants.

Whether its BDSM, tantric sex, or another kind of kinkiness that someone's into, what might be considered irregular sexual behavior is in the eye of the beholder. Someone who is empathetic could participate in any of the aforementioned forms of unconventional sex. The same holds true for a sexopath. The difference is in the intention behind the acts. It's not the action but the user that matters.

Indeed, when it comes to sexual behavior, external observations only get us so far. What we might think is weird, messed-up, frightening, or disgusting, might be fulfilling an important empathetic goal for both (or several) partners in a sexual experience. It also might be serving sexopathic ends for one of those involved. It all depends on what's going on internally—and that can even be a moving target when it comes to distinguishing between the empathetic person and the sexopath.

Temporary vs Permanent Sexopathy: Always Hurtful

Allie, our example at the beginning of the chapter, is not a sexopath. Whether her adultery can be written off as morally permissible isn't our concern. That's for Allie and her husband (if she chooses to tell him) to work out. What's relevant to us is how she was able to behave in a sexopathic manner, temporarily, even though she has empathy, a conscience, and feels remorse.

How can people who aren't sexopaths act like Allie? Are all affairs sexopathic? What about one-night stands? What if I were to tell you that the sex Allie was having with the man she met on the road was spiritual, life-altering sex? How would that change your perception of her behavior?

Having casual, no-strings-attached, friends-with-benefits, or carefree-sex doesn't make someone a sexopath. It *might* mean that someone is behaving in a sexopathic manner. Here is a rather extreme example: a guy is rebounding from a breakup and visits a strip club. At this particular strip club, the girls are not treated with the utmost respect by customers and staff. After this rebounding man gets a lap dance with one of them, the bouncer offers him a chance to have sex with her for a few hundred dollars even though the girl doesn't seem excited about the prospect. The rebounding man can be capable of temporarily turning his empathy off and forking that couple hundred over to have reluctant sex with the stripper. The man might regret it immediately afterward and never do anything of the sort again. He will have behaved sexopathically but wouldn't be a sexopath—on the contrary, he remains an empathetic person.

HORMONES UP

CONSCIENCE DOWN

Regret and remorse that often follow empathetic people after a drunken one-night stand isn't the sort of thing sexopaths experience—ever. Empathetic people might experience it in different ways. Some might be used to that sort of remorse that comes with their hangover and not give themselves too hard a time about the regrettable acts from the previous night. Others might swear to never drink again—or, at least, not go out immediately after a breakup.

Broadly speaking, men seek sexual fulfillment while many women seek romantic fulfillment. Guys exhibit sexopathic behavior, especially when they are younger, as the drive for sexual gratification overtakes all other thoughts. In seeking romantic fulfillment, a woman may want to be spoiled and pampered. She may want to be treated like a princess and showered with affection. However, when the fantasy is over, the fairy tale end is supposed to be happy for everyone. She wants her prince (or princess depending on her orientation) to be satisfied too. Pure sexual gratification, even when it is sought by women, is more about the personal release rather than a happily-ever-after for everyone.

Being inebriated—whether under the influence of drugs, alcohol, or one's own changing hormones—affects our ability to do everything: that includes empathizing. Even when well-rested, well-fed, and stone sober, a sexopath cannot empathize. They can never feel what another person feels. It's impossible.

What always matters is the intention behind the behavior. In that sense, people can fall into three main categories for our purposes: empathetic people, empathetic people who can behave in a temporarily sexopathic manner, and sexopaths. Understanding these three distinctions is important to understand the games true sexopaths play.

EMPATH   SEXOPATHIC BEHAVIOR   SEXOPATH

Chapter 3: Life is a Game - Did You Know You Were Playing?

David and Mark are in a bar. Unfortunately, this isn't a setup for a joke, unless you've got a dark sense of humor. This is a well-known gay bar in town, an institution. Openly gay men feel safe coming here and neither David nor Mark are shaky or uncertain about their sexuality. Both in their late thirties, each has been openly gay for more than a decade. Mark sees David at the other end of the bar picking at the label of his beer alone. He orders himself a drink, walks down, and slides into place at a bar stool beside David.

VULNERABLE EMPATHS =

SEXOPATH TARGETS

"Some weeks just seem like they go on forever," Mark announces. "Thank God it's Friday."

"You can say that again," David answers sheepishly.

"Which part?" asks Mark.

"Both," David answers.

It's the beginning of the night so the place hasn't really heated up yet. There are only a few customers apart from the two of them. The bartender arrives with Mark's drink, a martini.

"Cheers to that," Mark says.

David reluctantly knocks his half-full beer bottle against the rim of Mark's martini glass.The two know each other as acquaintances. This is a medium-sized city and the gay community isn't enormous. Inevitably, Mark's shown up at some of the same parties as David over the years and vice versa. They've also had brief conversations at the bar in the past.

Mark watches as David pulls his lips off his bottle after their end-of-the-week celebratory toast. Then, David sighs.

"What's eating at ya my friend?" Mark asks.

David shakes his head.

"I get it, I get it," Mark says. "Don't want to talk about it, but let's be honest, how do expect to survive the night in silence with a face as cute as yours—guys are going to come up and try to talk, so say what's on your mind now, so it doesn't come barreling out later when you don't want it to."

David considers Mark's words, looking up at him for an instant, then back at the beer in his hands, to resume picking at the label.

"Alright," Mark says after a moment passes. "I get it, you want to be alone. I'll oblige."

"Wait," David says as Mark stands up. "Sit back down."

Mark does as he's told, taking another sip from his martini.

"I'll tell you what's up, but only if you promise that a sad story isn't going to drag down your night."

David looks up at Mark's eyes as he sits back down, but now Mark's looking down at David's butt, pressed against the cushion.

"You know what I've found out?" Mark asks. "Somehow stories don't seem so sad once you've got someone else to share them with."

David looks back to his beer bottle, "Even ones about your meth-smoking daddy calling you for a loan?"

It's slight—almost unnoticeable unless you're paying close attention (which David isn't, wrapped up as he is in his melancholy)—but with David's revelation, Mark's lips curl into a tiny grin.

SEXOPATHS APPEAR FRIENDLY

TO GAIN EMPATHS' TRUST

The two launch into a full-blown discussion about David's father. It turns out he's been an addict for years. With his mother's passing away when he was a teenager, David's father sunk deep into depression and began to self-medicate. As the only child, David has been stuck with carrying his father's burden his entire adult life. He's constantly stuck between the strong feelings of love he felt for his father as a boy and the shame he feels whenever his name is brought up now. It's clear from their conversation that David doesn't talk much about this.

As David explains the small details of his father's life and his experience about living with an addict parent, Mark checks out. David, can't tell, of course. Mark is nodding his head, uttering small sounds and words to keep David going. Inside his own mind, however, Mark is having an entirely different conversation with himself.

Mark has badly wanted to sleep with David for a long time. Not that he's unique, many of the attractive guys who frequent the bar are on Mark's mental list of bodies to conquer. Mark's focus on David at the moment is down to taking advantage of an opportunity—sad guy at a bar all alone, early, this is the type of chance Mark would kill for.

It's not just the sex he's after, though that's a big part of it, it's the control. Mark gets off on zeroing in on a target and then manipulating him to do whatever he wants. Anyone can have sex. Mark could even pay for it if he wanted to, or he were desperate. It's the thrill of the hunt he enjoys and the possibility to add not just another conquest to his growing collection, but another action figure to play with whenever he's bored or uninspired. Mark has absolutely no concern about David's father or their relationship, besides in the vulnerability it signals. He doesn't care whether or not a bit of rough sex will put David in a worse mental position.

None of this is revealed in Mark's actions or his words. In fact, all the tracks of these sinister thoughts are quite well hidden. All of his words and actions seem so kind, even brave: who else actively wants to hear an acquaintance spout so deeply about personal problems? The more David talks, between taking sips of his beer, the more Mark's mind reels with all the fun he can have with such a tortured soul. To him, it's all a game to be played.

Just as they are each time he comes into this bar, every move that Mark has made thus far has been calculated. There was a reason he pretended to give up easily at first. There was even a reason he didn't order David a drink when he did. It's all a part of his plan and no detail is unaccounted for. The irony of alcohol being poured down David's throat as he tells his father's sad tale of substance abuse is not lost on Mark. It's pounced on.

When their conversation reaches a crux, David catches himself before talking too deeply about the showers he and his father took as a boy. Mark's fully locked in. He's not letting this one get away.

"How about I order another one of those," Mark suggests, pointing at David's empty beer bottle with the mangled label. "And you can tell me about it?"

Mark's been so nice all evening. He's such a good listener, somehow the depressing story doesn't further depress him. When it comes to a guy like Mark, David never really stood a chance.

"Sure," David says, flashing a grin for the first time all night—maybe the first time in weeks. "But why don't we make it a martini this time?"

Now Mark doesn't need to hide his smile. It's one anyone who's come into contact with a sexopath should recognize. It's the smile of victory.

SEXOPATH GAMES

The Game: Sociopathic Gamemaster, Empathetic Pawn

It's great to understand what sociopathy is (and is not) but it's even more important to recognize how it functions in the human brain. Inside the mind of a sociopath, the world is simply a game. You read that correctly. The whole world—the people, places, and things in it—are all a giant game board with movable pieces. Without an ability to empathize, the idea that there are others beside themselves playing this game is inconceivable. Sociopaths are the master and player of the game.

There are even some types of jobs which sociopaths would be more prone to taking because the careers provide them with a better opportunity to run up the score of the game. For example, sociopaths can make great firemen. They will rush in, endangering themselves, for the ego padding that comes with saving the day. They crave the accolades after and the thrill of the danger. They love to count the number of fires they put out and the people that they saved, but not because they care about the people.

COMMON SOCIOPATH JOBS

* Airport Security
* Ambulance Worker
* Chef
* Chief Executive Officer (CEO)
* Civil Servant
* Entrepreneur
* Fireman
* Hollywood Executive
* Journalist

* Lawyer
* Marketing
* Media Personality
* Police Officer
* Politician
* Religious Leader
* Salesperson
* Surgeon
* Temp Agency Worker

They will run into a burning building and singe their lungs for the prize. This is all without considering the sexual fantasies people have about sleeping with firemen and being rescued (from sexual dissatisfaction) by a brawny fireman. The saying goes, "Find 'em hot, leave 'em wet!" Being firemen could be a great profession for a sexopath.

SOCIOPATHS HAVE NO FEAR

TRUE HERO OR FEARLESS OPPORTUNIST?

A related field that sociopaths gravitate toward is that of emergency medical technician. These are the folks working on an ambulance. Sociopaths crave the adrenaline rush of saving someone without the emotional turmoil associated with witnessing another person's pain. Many EMTs become burned out after seeing such pain again and again. Not the sociopath. Their detached lack of empathy makes burnout less likely. You do not need to care about a person in order to perform effective CPR. In fact, too much caring may result in less effective chest compressions as an empathetic person will flinch as they crack the patient's ribs. A sociopath won't care. They only care about themselves—and the glory acting as the hero will bring. This is why a sociopath functions well in this profession, the ability to not care being an advantage in certain situations.

Sociopaths can also make great surgeons who are known for their poor bedside manner. Often to the surgeon, patients are merely diagnoses (the breast cancer in room 138, the appendectomy in 234) in bodies to cut. Sociopathic surgeons are unable to see the patient as a person, but rather see an opportunity to play God. When you are undergoing surgery, one would argue a steady hand is more important than empathy. Technical skill is more important than the ability to care. The sociopathic surgeon desires to win the game of successful surgery without distraction of the soul within the body whom they cut.

My steady hands are all the empathy I need

On the other hand, sociopaths do not do well in positions of power—although they often pursue them. Controlling others is the goal of their game, so sociopaths are drawn to positions where they can force others to do as they say. Oddly, sociopaths actually believe (or claim to believe—anything they say is suspect given their pathological lying) that society is better off when they are in control. A strong characteristic of sociopaths is a feeling of superiority. They see empathetic people as limited due to their conscience and being too caught up in their deep emotions to even understand there is a game to be won. Sociopaths think they are advancing society by taking over the world using deceptive charm and lies to advance their personal agendas.

Sociopaths believe they do very well in elected office but with them around, it is the people with a conscience and empathy who end up suffering. It has been said that in America today, you have to be a sociopath or psychopath in order to get elected. It has even been said that Jesus Christ would not stand a chance in a current election. When did lying politicians become the norm? Why do empathetic people continue to believe the lies? People who lie as easily as they breathe are not suited to a position where truthfulness and empathy are required.

Though this is by no means a comprehensive list, seeing some of the types of jobs sociopaths pursue and thrive in can help round out your understanding of the games sociopaths play. It's all about running up the score and, in the case of sexopaths, as much as they'd like to be having sex all the time, all that sex without the game isn't the same to them. The joy of winning fades away when it gets too easy or redundant. In the end, control beats out orgasm.

The Rules: Always Changing

The rules of this game are defined by the sociopath, of course. All the other pieces (aka people) are merely pawns to be manipulated. Victims are not seen as people but as objects. Often serial rapists see their victims simply as a sexual dumpster to satisfy themselves. With the ability (and propensity) to change the rules to better suit themseves at any time they choose, a picture of how unfair this game is should be starting to take shape. Since the rules are constantly changing (and there are really no rules about the rules) one way to think of them is in terms of how a sociopath might organize other people.

Most sociopaths divide the pawns they come across into three different groups. For sociopaths, the first group is people they think can be useful. This is the group where possible sex partners are organized. It's where sociopaths and sexopaths also place easily manipulated people, especially ones in their workplace or social life (these are great people to help them acquire more sexual targets). In some way, these are the people sociopaths and sexopaths focus their time and energy on—because they have some use to winning the game.

The second group is those who might be trouble. These are people who can disrupt or bother a sociopath's pursuit of the first group. For some reason, these people are either deliberately or accidentally standing in their way. While this category might include other sexual targets, some large barrier makes them not worth the trouble. This can include other rival sociopaths who might be competing over the same prizes. A sociopath will avoid or seek to destroy this group.

A sociopath will deem the third group unworthy, uninteresting, and irrelevant. In fact, they might not even realize they are dividing this group into a category at all, such is their blatant disregard for them. It's as if they don't see them at all. To a sociopath, these people aren't even part of the game. They are like painted-faces in a television background of a stadium crowd—just blotches of color that barely register as alive.

Ironically, it's this last group who can most easily identify the sociopath (or, at least, that there's a problem). We will talk more about this in Part II of the book, but the best time to spot sociopaths are when they aren't looking. Fortunately, sociopaths are so focused on their objectives there are inevitably blind spots.

The Objective: Win at All Costs

The objective of the sociopath's game is personal gain and satisfaction. It's that plain and that simple. Everything else in the life of sociopaths is secondary to this pursuit—including their own safety.

Sociopaths can be remarkable in their disregard for their own well-being. They will place themselves in precarious positions if it means a shot at getting a more pleasurable result in any current game they are playing. Though the approach internally is reckless, on the outside they appear cool as a cucumber. They always like to seem in control—it's part of the game.

It should go without saying at this point that sociopaths do not care about others. They don't care what happens to others, unless it can positively affect their pursuit of their objective: personal gain and satisfaction. While that satisfaction might vary slightly from sociopath to sociopath, for those sexopaths with hypersexuality and sex addiction, the type of satisfaction almost always being sought is of the sexual variety.

Personal gain and satisfaction – is that too much to ask?!

They need sex for their own survival, the way other people need food, water, and shelter. If they go without it for a prolonged period of time, they feel as if they are going to die. This isn't a case of someone just "getting their needs met." No. Remember, like drug addicts who will do anything to get high, these are sex addicts who will do anything to get their sexual fix.

It's the sociopathic or psychopathic part of the equation that differentiates them from the empathetic sex addicts who put their conscience on temporary hold to behave sexopathically. True sexopaths are capable of keeping the game up a lot longer than someone who doesn't have the sociopathic or psychopathic mind.

Sociopaths are calculated in their recklessness. They can be very strong tactically but frequently fail strategically because of their impulsivity. Their objectives are so important to them, that they take great care in attaining them. Sociopaths take winning seriously. They are professionals. If there were a league for this sort of behavior, team sociopath would win every year.

The Stakes: Everything You Hold Dear

The pursuit of these objectives will lead sociopaths down a path that can include crime, sexual misconduct, and even murder. In short: the games sociopaths play—their modus operandi—are not to be taken lightly. Of course, making this all the more difficult is the quintessential sociopathic tendency to constantly change the rules of the game to suit their whims and get them closer to winning.

What's at stake here are two of the biggest issues of our time: sexual harassment and rape. Sexopaths choose to be delusional. When challenged, they say they believe their victims actually enjoy sexual violation. They can convince themselves of this because of the lack of empathy they possess. When aroused, even temporary sexopaths are often incapable of feeling someone else's pain when it comes into conflict with their pleasure.

Some researchers have investigated why rape is so common among soldiers in war. The soldiers in question do, indeed, become temporarily sexopathic (if a given individual wasn't already a true sexopath to begin with). In their case, researchers have hypothesized that the presence of death leads to an evolutionary impulse to spread their seed. Basically, because death can come at any moment, rape becomes the quickest option for procreation and sexual satisfaction. Sexopaths on the whole also behave this way, if they aren't getting any sex, then what's the point of living? Life's purpose, to them, is to play the game to win it.

One great example of the kinds of sexopathic delusions that we've covered in this chapter is the character TenSin in my novel *69 Shades of Nashville*. TenSin is a politician who sets his sexopathic eyes on a fellow sexopath in NashvilleKitty. His domination of her in their encounter is so severe and violent, it qualifies as rape. The irony is that much of the way TenSin plays his game is the same as NashvilleKitty. Her displeasure and pain that derives from the situation, is simply a case of her being on the wrong end of winning. TenSin, of course, doesn't care. He actually believes she enjoyed it and will be back for more. He's as unable to understand her pain as she is to the pain she causes others. His mind, like hers and all the other sexopaths out there, is firmly focused on the game.

Chapter 4: Masked to the Max

Lisa is an elementary school teacher in her forties. Teaching in one of the nation's biggest cities has given her the chance to work at both public and private schools across a number of different socioeconomic areas. During her tenure of over two decades, she's taught at over a dozen different schools. In fact, she has a self-imposed rule to switch schools every couple of years. When asked by her colleagues—nearly all of whom are devastated to see her depart their school—about her reasons for changing schools so frequently, her response is always the same.

"After two years, I fall too much into a routine. I stop developing new plans to suit students' and familes' needs. I just can't bring my best self when I get too comfortable in an environment."

With responses like this, it's not hard to understand why her colleagues hate to see her go. Some of them, though, don't mind watching Lisa leave.

Lisa spends all the hours outside of school at the gym making sure to keep her body toned. If you ask the men at her school, they'll tell you she doesn't look at day over thirty. The women can't believe how soft the skin on her face appears. She has no crow's feet. There are no visible wrinkles from the smile that seems like it's permanently glued to her face.

It's not just her looks either. Lisa makes it a point to befriend members of the staff by learning their names within the first week of the school year. It doesn't matter if someone is male or female, young or old, Lisa gets to know them a bit and often memorizes their birthdays (she's prone to sneaking a little bag of freshly baked cookies to them on their special day).

On top of being conscientious, she's funny. She's always got the latest pop culture references at the ready for jokes during staff meetings and lunch breaks. Lisa is a shining light for even the grumpiest employees at the schools where she works. Even to her detractors, those who are jealous about the attention she receives wherever she goes, her charisma is undeniable.

Whenever Lisa leaves a school, the principal's office is flooded with visits and phone calls from parents of children Lisa's taught. They want to know where she went. They want to know why. They demand to know why the school didn't do more to keep her.

Where is all this coming from? Why does almost everyone seem to love Lisa? What's her secret?

Well, the one place you won't get an answer is from her students themselves. Lisa almost always chooses to teach fourth grade. To them, it's not that she's a bad teacher, she just doesn't seem totally present while she's teaching. She's not excellent at helping students until after parent-teacher conferences take place a quarter of the way through the school year. Even after those conferences, it always seems that she gives more attention to some students than others without regard for whether or not they are struggling in class. Lisa's not the worst teacher any of them have had, but she just seems to be on autopilot as far as they are concerned. The students struggle to understand why the adults—their parents and the other school employees—seem so thrilled by her.

What's all of this like from Lisa's perspective? Why does she do what she does? Where does she see herself in the conversations about her? Well, if we're going to find out, we have to take her mask off—quite literally in Lisa's case.

Since high school, Lisa's known she was different. The word she would use privately wouldn't be *different* though, it would be *better*. She grew up in a small town but escaped to the city as soon as she could.

SEXOPATHS MOVE OFTEN

Out with the old
In with the new
Who can I use?
Who can I screw?

TO FIND NEW PREY

This was mostly because she had sexually explored every person she felt attracted to in her town before she could drive. Male or female, it has never made a difference to Lisa—a body is a body, and the potential for thrill and satisfaction is always possible given the right set of criteria.

Once she arrived in the city, she entered community college and began to explore different options for a career that would give her the highest possibilities for varied, repeated, high-grade sexual experiences. Teaching was not an option that was on her radar until she met a professor in one of her classes. The woman was charismatic, just like Lisa. She was beautiful, just like Lisa. She was also a master at manipulation just like Lisa. The student was happy to let the teacher manipulate her until they found themselves in a sixty-nine position beneath the desk after a late-night class one evening.

Once Lisa revealed to the professor her true colors, the professor was happy to fill her in with the secrets about why she should choose teaching as a position (she only delivered these lessons in return for sexual favors, of course). Teaching allowed for interfacing with multiple potential sexual partners on a weekly, if not a daily, basis. Students had a vested interest in getting on teacher's good sides so could be more open to sexual pursuits. The best part was that they would be gone in a few months, with an entire new group to replace them.

"I keep getting older and bolder, they stay the same age and malleability," the professor told Lisa.

It turned out, teaching was a great option for Lisa. The best part? She didn't even need to bother with waiting to get credentialed. The professor knew someone who produced fake degrees. As long as Lisa was willing to take on a new name and bump her age up a few years, she could be ready to enter the employment market the next year.

The professor warned her to stay out of the community college circuit, or if she wanted that age group to switch cities, because that was her territory. By then though, Lisa had already gotten what she needed out of the professor. She'd also thought up a way to multiply the number of potential sexual partners by simply choosing a different age bracket to focus on.

BIRDS OF A FEATHER MANIPULATE TOGETHER-

Wanna be the teacher's pet?

Anything for an easy A!

UNTIL THEY DON'T

She chose elementary school as it gave even more options for sexual satisfaction. Every kid had two parents. The fourth-grade age bracket was also one where the parents were starting to see their marriages fray and more prone to seek sexual satisfaction elsewhere, without actively looking for divorces (the older the children got, the more likely their parents couldn't stand each other any longer). She crunched all these numbers and tested her theories during her first year of teaching (where she began as a substitute teacher for every grade).

After she realized fourth grade was the golden age group to find the kinds of parents she was looking for, the last piece of the puzzle came with a risky experience she had at one school. The first two years flew by—she was having a great time, juggling multiple parents and even a faculty member or two—but as she was beginning her third year, too many of her side-pieces started demanding more attention. Some of them had multiple kids and when she tried to shake them off, another kid would come along, and she'd be forced to sit in parent-teacher conferences long after her thirst for the parent in question had already been quenched. That's when she instituted her two-year-per-school rule. It also helped that since she was teaching the same grade at a different school, she could simply reuse all her material for class and focus her mental energy on manipulating everyone in the equation (parents, staff, students) toward her own sexual ends.

Lisa is a full-blown sexopath. However, the reason she's been able to operate in the clear for all these years, is because she is an expert at designing her mask. Along with the lack of empathy and the game, the mask is an integral part of the sociopath's makeup—and it's often the only thing those of us on the outside ever see.

Hiding in Plain Sight

Sociopaths, as the example of Lisa indicates, can seem to be complex, hard to identify people. They can be extremely intelligent and fun to be around. They are charming, and they do a great job at tricking people into not suspecting anything about their true motives. In that way, they are hiding in plain sight.

How can they do this? What makes it even possible? Shouldn't we be able to see or sense these people wandering among us?

Unlike empathetic people, sexopaths don't have the option of just avoiding people to protect themselves. Because they are always looking for other sexual partners, they are forced, constantly, to be out in public. Usually, they like to keep a fairly large stable of options at their disposal. Even if they choose to do most of their hunting online, they know that you can only get so far digitally. Physical contact isn't just necessary—it's the whole goal.

They need to be constantly meeting new people and, at the same time, concealing their true intentions. This puts the sexopath in a difficult position (not that they mind those much). For all intents and purposes, this conundrum isn't one that will ever go away for them. For the rest of their lives, they will have to figure out a way to square this circle. They have no choice but to construct a mask for themselves.

The Physical Mask

With the goal to keep manipulating people and adding to their stable of sexual partners and possibilities, sexopaths need to increase their odds of not being discovered. To stack the deck in their favor, sexopaths and

SOCIOPATHS HAVE A DIFFERENT

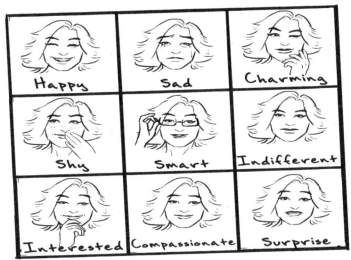

MASK FOR EVERY OCCASION

sociopaths employ a number of techniques but many can be summarized in one idea: the mask. Whether it's superficial charm, intelligence, apparent altruism, or an uncanny charisma, sociopaths use their mask to hide their true intentions, both verbally and nonverbally.

Lisa, the example at the beginning of the chapter, exhibits every aspect of a well-developed mask. She's fully committed. Everything in her life is carefully-added detail to the mask. From her teaching credentials and phony identification papers (which make her appear many years numerically older than she actually is) to the amount of money she's invested in plastic surgery to make her face appear younger, more-innocent, child-like and desirable, Lisa organizes her entire existence around maintaining her mask because it's the key for her to get what she wants, her life's purpose: sexual satisfaction.

Of course, making oneself as attractive as possible is a big part of any sexopath's mask. It's not just the plastic surgery and Botox that Lisa's invested in. She purchases the most expensive and effective cosmetics. She eats well. She exercises regularly. It goes without saying that regular bathing and grooming are a big part of Lisa's routine. There is a good reason why normally only attractive people star on television and in movies. Other people find attractiveness attention-grabbing and—as insane as this sometimes seems—reason enough to trust someone. Sexopaths have no choice but to try to maximize their attractiveness by obscuring their fewer desirable features and accentuating their best ones.

Simply exercising, getting plastic surgery, or using make-up does not, obviously, automatically make someone a sexopath. These things are optional, if sometimes recommended, for empathetic people. For sexopaths they are requirements. These are boxes that must be checked if they are going to hope to succeed in their mask-building.

The Personality of the Mask

Any mask for a sociopath is much more than its mere physical composition. Favorable personality traits are applied to the exterior like layers of paint on a mural. Intelligence, though it does exist in and of itself, is much easier to fake than most people think. Sociopaths, who are often good at brief, intense focus, take well to rote memorization and can easily regurgitate a set of preloaded facts to impress a new colleague or social connection. They often have a superficial knowledge of many topics adding to their worldly façade.

Charisma is also a trait that can be easily faked. Knowing in their minds that they are not representing their true selves, sociopaths can easily pretend to be an imagined person—even taking on a full separate identity. Being charismatic as someone else can be far easier than acting as your true self and maintaining a high level of charm. Need evidence? Look no further than the big screen, where even the most socially awkward actors can become different people for months at a time while filming in order to fool an audience. Sociopaths operate in much the same way, by pretending to be someone they are really not and doing a better job at it than if they had to simply be themselves.

Altering the mask to suit the situation is also part of a sociopath's charm. Sociopaths change their masks as often as the debutant changes clothes. By focusing on what one individual wishes to see reflected back, a sociopath is able to paint the picture of the instant soul mate or perfect friend. Often, they will start with a seemingly very personal story (that is often a complete lie) to let you think they are really opening up to you and to make you believe it is safe for you to respond in kind with an equally personal tale. They will ask innocent-seeming questions to obtain more information and parrot back to you what you say, making you think that they agree with everything you believe. It will seem like they are incredible listeners who truly care about you and what you have been through, but be warned, they are actually collecting data on your vulnerabilities to be used to their advantage at a later time.

Sociopaths also choose to appear friendly or helpful to others. Altruism, like in the case of Lisa, is one surefire characteristic for a sociopath to cultivate by showing a personality that will throw detractors off the scent of exposing them for who they really are. Lisa's seemingly altruistic concern for the betterment of students is something she points to when people ask her why she's leaving for other schools. She appears to be an incredibly gracious and giving person to outsiders who imagine what it must be like to move from school to school so often. In their eyes she does it all for the kids, when nothing could be further from the truth. Hence, her mask is incredibly well-conceived and her behavior well-executed. Even the chosen occupation of an educator bolsters Lisa's mask because, like a doctor, it's a job that has a reputation of people who care deeply for others, even when the opposite is the case for her.

These are just a few examples of the kinds of personality traits with which sociopaths can paint their mask. In the end, what's depicted depends on the sociopath. Even more important than the physical and personality construction of the mask is the story that glues it all together.

Ditto!

SOCIOPATHS REPEAT BACK
WHAT YOU WANT TO HEAR

The Story Behind the Mask (aka The Legend)

While every sociopath will create a mask, only the most skilled ones will also create a foolproof story to go along with it. Since these masks—in both the physical sense and the personality—are fabrications, it's possible for cracks to appear, for a sociopath to be uncovered. That's why any good mask comes with a good story.

Everyone has a story and sociopaths need one too to make them appear as real, 3D-humans to their targets. Often the story will change in the telling from individual to individual or group to group depending on what best suits the sociopath. For example, when a colleague asks Lisa how she shows up with a smile every day on her face, she is prepared with an "over-the-top" story about her grandfather who was always hesitant to smile until the day he had his teeth knocked out in a bull-riding accident. The surgery on his mouth that followed, Lisa might say, left him without the ability to smile at all. For all his grandchildren, the grandfather would constantly instill the necessity to smile every day as if it was the last smile you could ever give—a gift, because that's what he realized when it was too late.

Though it's just one small example, these are the types of cheesy back stories that sociopaths must develop if they are going to convince people their mask is real, or rather, to have a mask good enough to where people would never guess something is awry. Of course, the delivery is just as important. That's where a sociopath has to execute their loose understanding of the truth.

I don't exist, but I'm a great story!

SOCIOPATHS CREATE OVER-THE-TOP BACK STORIES

4 OUT OF 5 DENTISTS AGREE, LYING DOES NOT COUNT AS FLOSSING

Half-Truths and Lies: Words of Manipulation

Truth is much more fluid in a sociopath's world. Remember, sociopaths look like everyone else. Lying comes as easily as breathing to them, and they can even beat a polygraph machine as they do not have an increase in heart rate, blood pressure, or perspiration while they deceive.

Perhaps there is no action a sociopath does that better explains the function of the story of the mask than half-truths. Though many of us have told these sorts of partial-lies in our lives (when someone asks if they look good in something or some relative pries about whether we like their holiday gift or not), this tool is a sociopath's expertise. A well-crafted mask will help them lie without being detected and to tell half-truths that conceal their non-altruistic desires.

Lisa delivered a great half-truth in her response to those who asked why she switches schools so often. She said, "After two years, I fall too much into a routine. I stop developing new plans to suit students' and families' needs. I just can't bring my best self when I get too comfortable in an environment."

This is a brilliant half-truth because what Lisa is really talking about is her sex life. On the surface, this seems like the type of altruistic remark her colleagues have come to expect of her. In fact, it's her sexual partners that have become too routine. She doesn't develop new plans to sleep with students' family members because she has already slept with all of them, or they now bore her, or they are getting too close to her. She's not being her best sexopathic self anymore because her environment is too comfortable (or stale) for her. Half-truths like these not only serve the mask they spout out of, they also manage to keep sexopaths and sociopaths hidden directly in plain sight.

In my novel, *69 Shades of Nashville*, NashvilleKitty is an expert at wielding her mask. She applies it easier than most women can apply makeup for the day. NashvilleKitty is much like Lisa. They are both using their well-crafted masks to calculate the quickest route between themselves and their goal of satisfaction and personal gain.

Seeing Past the Mask - The Hidden Truth

Some sociopaths are more adept than others when creating this mask (its physical features, the personality behind it, and a story to hold it all together), while others are better at keeping it up all the time. Some sexopaths are reckless enough with their mask that they only show it to people they plan to sleep with. Around others, their mask slips off, allowing the community at large to identify the true characters of these people even if their targets cannot.

Other sociopaths are better at keeping the mask on, managing to keep it up during most social interactions. However, much as they would like to believe otherwise, no sociopath is perfect when it comes to keeping a flawless mask up at all times. There are several ways to see through even a well-crafted sociopathic mask.

One way to spot a sociopath is to watch them closer than they are watching you. Preferably watch the sociopath when they do not realize they are being observed. A sociopath with enough intelligence can create a normal-appearing mask, but even a sociopath cannot maintain it all the time.

SOCIOPATH WATCHES DOG RUN OVER

WATCH FOR THE DELAY IN FAKING EMPATHY

In short, pay close attention to the mask—and the face—itself. If you suspect someone of being a sociopath monitor closely for micro-inflections of empathy. Often the sociopath will lack the subtle physical signs of empathy or the micro-inflections become macro-inflections when they attempt to mimic empathy and their movements are greater than the unconscious facial changes of the empathetic soul. Sociopaths do not have automatic empathy complete with corresponding facial expressions like the rest of us. They must figure out how society expects them to respond and then put on the proper facial expression for the situation.

The best way to go about these sorts of observations is in groups. Not only can other people help you get a better sense of someone by asking them questions you might not think to ask or by noticing something you might have missed, but they also give you the chance to step back from the relationship. It is harder for sociopaths to tailor their masks to each individual in a group so often cracks in the façade are evident.

Quality observation means trying to look at someone objectively. Like a scientist with a clipboard watching a police investigation behind a one-way mirror, you can finally watch for patterns without worrying about whether you are being manipulated during the course of a conversation. As an observer instead of a participant, you can start making some behavior connections of your own and detailing mental (or physical) notes of what you've seen. Without varying the kinds of settings when you see someone and the people you see them with, this sort of observation is nearly impossible. When potential sociopaths control the environment, letting them run the show is only playing into their hands. Shake it up. You cannot get to know someone if your relationship is one-dimensional.

Along with the understanding of a complete lack of sexual empathy with no conscience and the desire to manipulate others in their game of life, this mask is the last of the three ingredients essential to a basic understanding of sexopathy. But like all things academic and ideological, the point is how it applies to the real world, which is the goal of Part II.

SHHHH.....YOU DON'T SEE ME

Part II: Staying Safe in a Sexopathic World

Chapter 5: Glimpse Behind the Mask: Before It's Too Late

Chloe had got herself into a pickle, and she knew it. For six months, she had been working with a new partner at the law firm. His name was Larry. As a paralegal, Chloe was at the behest of the partners—doing everything from important case work during discovery, carrying files to court, and getting coffee for her bosses. One thing she hadn't realized was included in her available services to Larry and the other partners was her body.

Larry was a hotshot lawyer recently hired from a competing firm after he promised to bring several large clients with him. The law firm was lucky to have him—and he knew it. He acted like he owned the place. Everyone was buzzing about the attractive new guy since he arrived. Even the female junior partner cast him an admiring look.

"Isn't she engaged?" Chloe thought. "It doesn't matter. I'm staying out of it."

Chloe had aspirations to be a lawyer herself and was taking night classes toward her law degree. At the same time, she was focused on getting her current legal work done and done well. The firm had been very supportive of her future legal plans and nothing could distract her from reaching her dreams—including office gossip about the new guy.

It was business as usual for Chloe, at least until Larry began to stare at her. This wasn't the normal, friendly (or even flirtatious) kind of stare either. They would be sitting in a meeting, and Larry's eyes would fall onto Chloe and stay there for far longer than she felt was appropriate. It wasn't as though he was looking at her in the eyes, either. His pupils focused on her chest when she was sitting at the table with him, or she'd catch them glued to her backside when she leaned down to gather files from the stacks on the floor. It's not that she hadn't been gawked at before. Since she was in high school, Chloe was aware she had the kind of shape where construction workers and football players alike would whistle when she walked by. She used to be embarrassed by it but had grown comfortable with her figure. That is, until Larry began eyeing her.

What is even more strange about these moments of obtrusive staring was that he looked upon her with a sort of absent, mindless focus. It reminded Chloe of the way people gaze off into the distance when they are thinking about something really hard and they—for all intents and purposes—disappear from their physical bodies and are lost in thought. It was just like that, Chloe thought, except the distance he stared off into was her cleavage or rear panty line. He was undressing her with his eyes.

These stares made Chloe feel uncomfortable, but as the months passed, they became the new normal. She came to expect it at work, doing her best to ignore his unblinking gaze and, in her own way, vanish into her duties. After all, she understood the corporate environment and retaliation of tattle-tales, so reporting Larry to colleagues or Human Resources could only compromise her march toward her career goals. As annoying as Larry was, she kept her mouth shut.

He's a jerk, but I've got a job to do. I'm stuck.

Then, quite suddenly, the staring stopped. She didn't notice it at first. What surprised her was the uptick in Larry's verbal communication. During the staring period, they had hardly spoken to each other. He occasionally asked her for a file or a cup of coffee, but for the most part their conversations were minimal. Suddenly, he began asking her questions about legal proceedings or requesting her opinion regarding various aspects of a case. His interest and inquiries startled her so much, that it took a few days to realize he'd actually stopped staring at her in that distant way and had begun simply glancing in her direction much as her boyfriend had before they broke up a year earlier.

Since they seemed to be building a rapport, she didn't deflect the personal attention he gave her. She had no intention of anything beyond a professional relationship but hearing the occasional compliment and being asked seemingly innocent personal questions was a nice change of pace for Chloe from the stuffy, all-business atmosphere the firm always seemed to promote. Larry would say, "Really sharp suit you're wearing" or "How's Smokie the cat faring?" on a daily basis with a kind of charm she felt lifted her mood.

The weird part about Larry—Chloe came to discover—was that on the work front, he seemed to be constantly dropping the ball. As a paralegal, part of her job was to cover the tracks of the lawyers by reviewing documents they'd prepared for a case. Almost without fail, Larry's work needed the most editing and correction. He made silly mistakes that she had never encountered at the firm or even heard of during her classes. She couldn't decide whether the errors came down to his rushing through things, if he had a genuine lack of understanding about certain basic legalese, or if he simply didn't care enough to be careful. Anytime the mistakes came up during meetings, he would deflect responsibility or find a way to accuse the other paralegals—but never Chloe—of negligence. It was odd behavior compared to everything else she observed of Larry. She didn't know whether he was someone to admire or be wary of—and she constantly swayed back and forth between those two poles inside and outside the office.

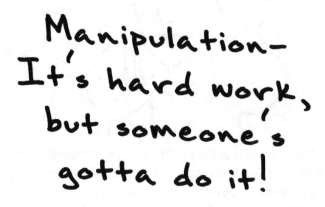

Larry's appreciation of Chloe grew, and he requested she be dedicated to his exclusive use while he worked on several important, time-sensitive cases. It turned out the clients he brought with him came with a huge load of work as well. The firm hired more people, but Human Resources couldn't catch up to the increased caseload. Even working solely for Larry, Chloe had more tasks than she could handle and decided to take a leave of absence from her classes until things slowed down. Her nights switched from studying cases to working on them with various colleagues from the office, including Larry.

Larry and Chloe often worked with a group at various late-night restaurants around their building. Chloe didn't mind working late as long as she didn't starve. Of course, the work during meals would often lag and the group strayed into conversation about life outside their cases. Chloe noticed how Larry wouldn't participate too much in the conversations unless she or her other younger, attractive colleagues did. She wondered whether all the women had received the same treatment from Larry from staring to friendly banter. After one marathon session, Chloe almost asked her paralegal equal and friend, Maureen, about it but then decided against it.

Slowly, as the swamp of work and long hours grew, the late-night group shrank until only Chloe and Larry remained. It was during that period, when it was just the two of them, that Larry's subtle flirtations morphed into overt advances.

First, he showered her with compliments and told her how much he admired her exceptional brain, legal skills and, yes, exquisite body. Chloe was flattered but conflicted. With school looking like a distant option, she worried that if she made a misstep at the office with Larry, she might mess up her career. At the same time, she was attracted to his high powered and successful lawyer status. He did seem to have a charming side and the more they spoke, the more they seemed to have in common. "We make a good team," she thought.

One night after work, Larry even told her the most heartwarming story about his ex-girlfriend. It turned out, his ex became addicted to prescription drugs and turned their relationship into a rollercoaster. Even though he felt the behavior surrounding her addiction was against the way he was raised, Larry did everything he could to help her kick her habit, "I even signed her up for experimental therapy sessions and started an exercise regimen with her to help her see the good side of normal life," he said. He stuck by her as long as he could, but in the end, she became psychotic and had to be committed to a mental institution.

The next week, emboldened by Larry's story and feeling so much more comfortable with him, Chloe finally divulged her own experiences about her ex-boyfriend of five years. "We had so many problems from the way we were raised," she said. "He was a liberal from the Northwest while my family was Midwest conservative."

As she shared her story, Larry was so kind and compassionate. The craziest part? It turned out Larry also was with his ex for five years, and he too grew up in the Midwest with a conservative family. To Chloe, their serendipitous coming together now seemed like love. This was meant to be. She was falling for him, fast.

Larry and Chloe had so many connections—it was like he could read her mind. But that wasn't all. As they grew closer, Larry would text her in the morning when she woke up and before she'd go to bed at night. He'd comment on her social media posts, showering her with compliments and attention. From all the stories Chloe heard about soul mates, she had never expected hers to appear right beside her at the office. It was almost an instant total connection, like she dreamt up the perfect partner and friend. Then, to top it all off, she started to get gifts from him at work—a pair of earrings for her favorite blue suit, a basket filled with expensive gourmet goodies to tide them over during long after hours, and even tickets to bands she liked. He also hinted that with their amazing soul connection, he was ready to step up the relationship.

It was all so intense, she hardly had time to make sense of it. Larry would tell her how much more he appreciated her than his crazy, drug-addicted ex. She totally understood his outpouring of affection could be attributed to his finally being with someone sane and with whom he shared so many connections. She imagined he felt as fulfilled as she did when they spent time together.

She thought back to when all she could think of was his most recent stare—not the first months of his gawking at her body, nor the flirtatious glances, but the way he looked at her that night at the restaurant, the first night they slept together. Over the rims of their cocktail glasses, he gazed deep into her eyes. She remembered how he didn't even bat an eyelid. Chloe blinked and looked away. She even asked, "Why are you looking at me that way?" With every movement, with every answer, he maintained the stare—until they at last left and went to his loft.

That first night Chloe slept with Larry, things happened so quickly, she hardly could keep track of the details. First, Larry used the excuse that since his loft was within walking distance from the office, they could just "crash for a few hours" and walk back to work in the morning to finish a particularly brutal casework.

IDEALIZATION

Later that night, after he gave her a tour of his modern bachelor pad and they shared a bottle of champagne, she let Larry slide off her clothes. He started slowly but with his incredible foreplay, she realized this sex was the best she ever had. He took control and delighted in tying her up, making her climax again and again. It was like nothing she had ever experienced before. Paired with all the other connections, the sexual chemistry seemed like the cherry on top of her match made in heaven.

Chloe couldn't believe how lucky she was. She even overlooked some of Larry's bizarre lies, telling her friends and family all his good points and that he was "the one." Although, they were happy for her and couldn't wait to meet him, they were destined to be disappointed. Every time Larry and Chloe made plans to introduce him to her friends or family, something always came up.

Just before a long weekend, Larry surprised Chloe with a jewelry box containing a sliver heart necklace centered with a tiny diamond. If she didn't have a year lease on her apartment, she would have moved in with him then and there. Of course, in their almost perfect realtionship, there was the issue of Smokie—Chloe's 21-pound Maine Coon cat. Larry swore that animals usually loved him, but Smokie hated Larry. The gigantic cat greeting him with menacing growls and outstretched claws the one time Larry visited Chloe's apartment. This meant that they spent most of their time at his loft. Chloe would check on Smokie daily, making sure he had enough food and water, while the happy couple concentrated on other things.

Life was so glorious with Larry, the adored and adoring lover, companion, and friend, Chloe even began to image wedding bells and a glorious white gown. There was a bridal shop two blocks from work with the most fabulous dress, complete with Alencon lace, beading and pearls, displayed in the window. The saleswoman gushed it was a designer gown for a non-designer price and that it would look absolutely perfect on Chloe with her incredible figure. Would she like to make a deposit?

Glancing at her ring-less hand, Chloe smiled and said, "Not yet. Maybe very soon."

After two weeks of perfect bliss, Chloe discovered that even paradise can have some blips. Having spent long hours at the office working on the case, Larry turned to Chloe and said, "I'm exhausted and just need to crash. Besides, I've been selfish taking all your time. I bet jealous Smokie would like to share you for a bit."

Chloe went back to her apartment which she had been visiting on daily 5-minute sprees to replenish the cat's necessities and lavished her pet with hugs, kisses, and scratches. Smokie, being a tolerant cat, forgave her after a few minutes of haughty displeasure. Perhaps it was the smell of Larry on her clothes that initially upset him.

The next day, back at the office, perfection once again reigned—almost. It was just a little thing, a minor glitch in one of her research pages, but Larry pointed it out in front of everyone. Of course, he was under such stress at work, Chloe could understand how he might snap at her.

That night, Chloe and Larry slept together without sex. She marveled at how content she was to simply lie next to him and decided to cook him a special dinner the next night. She would show him how wonderful their lives could be together as dreams of wedding bells occupied her thoughts.

Chloe cooked a spectacular meal with medium rare roast beef, fresh vegetables, and baked Alaska for dessert. Larry ate every bite and asked, "Why can't we have meals like this every night?" Still, he seemed happy with her and sex afterwards was glorious. Just before falling asleep, Larry murmured, "You know, I don't think Maureen likes me very much. I really wish you wouldn't spend time with her."

Desperate to please him and restore the honeymoon days of their romance, Chloe dedicated herself to being the perfect paralegal at work and the ideal partner in the loft. Leaving work, she raced first to her lonely apartment to throw food and water at Smokie. Then, she flew to the loft to fix dinner and to slip into something sexy. Meanwhile, Larry arrived sometimes hours later, saying he'd been at the bar with potential clients, working on more business so the firm would never forget how valuable he was.

As hard as Chloe tried, more little cracks kept bubbling up in their relationship. It seemed like no matter what she did, he still wasn't happy with her. She slaved over scrumptious desserts. He commented that her perfect figure was getting a bit pudgy around the edges. She really should start working out. The blue suit that he first saw her in and had said perfectly matched her eyes was getting a bit frayed and out of style. She should probably donate it to Goodwill.

SEXOPATHS MAKE YOU QUESTION YOUR SANITY

Chloe had found perfection in a relationship, and she wasn't giving up. That white gown was going to be hers as she walked down the aisle into her happily ever after—even if it killed her. Whatever he wanted, she desperately tried to give him. She canceled plans in order to always be available when he called. Catching the scent of another woman on him, she believed him when he claimed she was being "crazy and overly sensitive." He was too busy for affairs. She had no right to complain. She just tried harder.

The months rolled on and oddly enough, the more Chloe worked on trying to be flexible to accommodate his schedule, the more it started to backfire. The non-stop love and admiration she was used to began turning off and on like a light switch. One minute he was there, the next he was gone. The effect was jarring and made Chloe feel like her emotions were out of her control. She started to think that maybe he had lost interest in her, but then, to make matters even more confusing, Larry suddenly would show up with a gift or surprise her with a last-minute romantic weekend away.

Maureen stopped by her desk at work, worried by the frenzied and frantic look in her friend's eyes. Chloe was petrified that Larry would see them together. She whispered, "Meet me in the bathroom." At least the ladies' restroom was safe from Larry—unless he went into the men's room next door and could listen through the walls. What if he saw them exit together?

"You're being paranoid, Chloe," Maureen exclaimed. "Look what he's doing to you. You've cut your night classes and now you're terrified he'll catch you speaking to anyone else. He's driving you crazy—and he's not worth it!"

"He is! He is worth it! He is my soul mate," Chloe whispered. "You just don't know. You don't understand. It is all very complicated."

Maureen pointed out that even though Chloe spent less and less time with Larry, she loved him more and more. All Chloe could offer was that she felt confident in their relationship and every kind text or sweet compliment she received from Larry became more powerful than they were before. She felt herself craving his attention more than she had in any relationship and found herself practically stalking him on social media. He had become her world.

Unfortunately, Larry's constantly criticizing of Chloe's weight, appearance, cooking, and cleaning skills just got worse. Even her work as a paralegal was no longer up to his standards—not even close to the new paralegal the firm just hired. He subtly belittled Chloe's intelligence and abilities. His teasing seemed harmless from the outside, but internally she was devastated. Chloe felt like she was walking on eggshells. She never knew what would upset Larry next, and it seemed like no matter what she did, it was never good enough. To make matters worse, he claimed she was all "crazy-sensitive" after he posted some inside joke about an ex-girlfriend. Why had she acted that way? She could feel him pulling away. Chloe had messed up the best thing she ever had—and she couldn't figure out how or why. She wondered whether she indeed was going crazy.

Larry didn't always make it to dinner and sometimes, when he did, he was a little too drunk to enjoy it properly. Chloe tried not to pay too much attention to his drinking, but then she uncovered a cabinet at Larry's loft full of prescription bottles with his name on them. What else was he keeping from her? Frantic, she peeked at Larry's phone and found incoming texts from another woman.

With self-righteous anger, she confronted Larry about everything one night. Completely ignoring the cheating accusations, Larry blamed Chloe for his uptick in drinking and his need to get prescriptions to even himself out. When Chloe pressed Larry about the prescriptions and his ex-girlfriend's problems with them in the past, he exploded. "I was the one with the medication problems not my ex-girlfriend." Larry, in tears, screamed at Chloe his sob story about how his ex-girlfriend's cheating had pushed him to get hooked on pills. Confused, she pressed about whether this was the same girlfriend whom he dated for five-years that he had problems with because he was from the Midwest. He looked at her like she was the crazy one, reminding her that he was from New York and he had never seen a woman for more than a year in his life. At the end of the worst fight they had ever had, he blamed Chloe for her insensitivity and cruelty for even bringing it up. Chloe left the loft with Larry's claiming that he would not see her again until she could "learn to keep the drama in check." More than anything, he wanted peace and quiet.

At this point, Chloe was a complete emotional mess. She had no idea what was true and what wasn't. Had she heard him wrong all those months ago about his ex-girlfriend? Was she, in fact, going crazy?

DEVALUE

One evening, Larry came in 4 hours after work reeking of alcohol and cheap perfume. He announced that he simply couldn't continue this relationship any longer because Chloe had become too emotionally unstable. It simply was not good for his mental health, so he needed to put himself first and move on. With a dismissive wave, he tossed her few possessions and the clothes she had stored at his loft on the floor. "You have 5 minutes to get your crap before I call security. Hand over your key and get out."

Soon, he was posting pictures of a new happy couple all over social media. It turns out he appreciated not only the new paralegal's legal work but also her curvaceous body. Somehow, he convinced the entire office that Chloe was crazy. She was put on a performance improvement plan and moved to a different department. She felt completely confused as to what had happened. Where had she gone wrong? Despite all she tried to give Larry, Chloe was left worse off than she had ever been in her life: completely raped of emotion and floundering from her loss of dignity and self-worth. Her path to emotional redemption would be long in coming. It will take all her strength to overcome the devastation caused by Larry, the sexopath.

DISCARD

SEXOPATHS THROW YOU OUT WHEN DONE

The Sexopath Spotting Tool: Don't Leave Home Without It

Why have a sexopath spotting tool? It is not meant to make a diagnosis. That requires a medical professional trained in the evaluation process and takes hours to complete. Meanwhile, the general public needs a screening tool now in order to protect themselves from sexopaths, sociopaths and psychopaths in their lives. The Sexopath Spotting Tool is not designed to make a diagnosis but to identify behavior and determine how someone who might be a threat should be observed.

Getting to know people is not a matter of simply discovering their favorite color, where they went to high school, or their daily habits or routines. Among other things, it means delving into how deep their empathy is and whether they have a conscience. In real life situations, when and for what reasons do the empathetic connections cease to exist (or never work in the first place) and the reptilian brain takes over? Does the charming new acquaintance change into a callous, calculating stranger after two bottles of beer? After a shot of heroin? After a really hot woman or man walks into the room?

To that end, The Sexopath Spotting Tool helps identify certain traits in a person that may spell out a pattern of sexopathic behavior. It does not provide a psychological diagnosis, nor is it to be used as a means to conduct a witch hunt. I merely offer this tool to help people decide how they would like to proceed when they interact with certain individuals who might have sociopathic or sexopathic tendencies. Forewarned is forearmed.

For example, you may be in a relationship with someone and be disturbed when your partner fails to show the same amount of empathetic capabilities as you. The person fails to offer the compassion that you need, and you feel disappointed by their lack of support. Actions and words appear confusing and on opposite ends of reality. The Sexopath Spotting Tool can be useful to consider when deciding if you want to move forward with your emotional commitment to this person. Continuing to pour your love into a person incapable of returning your emotion is setting yourself up for a potentially devastating disappointment.

Do you know a Sexopath?

GLIMPSE BEHIND
THE MASK
A Sexopath Spotting Tool

Guiltless* - lack guilt, no remorse, no conscience
Lies* - lie as easily as they breathe, pathological
Infidelity - many relationships using deception
Manipulative* - life is a game, people are pawns
Predatory stare* - unblinking, see people as prey
Sexopath love cycle - idealize, devalue, discard
Empathy lacking* - can't feel what others feel

Break the law* - think rules do not apply to them
Egotistical* - narcissistic, feel entitled, glib
Hollow emotions* - cold, callous, no fear/love/worry
Irresponsible* - unreliable, parasitic lifestyle
Not me* - never their fault, blame others/situation
Danger seekers* - hate boredom, want thrills

Targeting next sexual victim - always on the prowl
Head honcho* - use power to manipulate others
Expressional inconsistencies* - fake emotions, mask

Magnetism *- superficial charm, mirror back to fool
Anger* - fits of illogical rage over trivial things
Sex addiction - often about control/conquest
Kill for power and control* - want to win at all costs

*True for sociopath or psychopath with or without sex addiction

GLIMPSE BEHIND THE MASK:
The Sexopath Spotting Tool

The Sexopath Spotting Tool has several items specific to sexopaths—sociopaths or psychopaths with a sex addiction—but the majority of the traits apply to sociopaths and psychopaths with or without this specific trait. This tool will teach the common character traits of people without a conscience who are incapable of empathy. The characteristics that apply to all sociopaths, psychopaths, and sexopaths are clearly marked. I have combined these characteristics into a mnemonic which is a memory technique using the first letter of each trait in a phrase: GLIMPSE BEHIND THE MASK. I was actually called the "Mnemonic Queen" in medical school so coming up with a 20 letter mnemonic which so aptly describes this personality type was a fun challenge. Each character trait begins with a telling quote from NashvilleKitty in my novel *69 Shades of Nashville* revealing the inner workings of a sexopath's mind. Let's delve into the meaning of each letter with this more detailed description:

Guiltless*
*applies to sociopaths, psychopaths, and sexopaths

> *The unified self allows me to act and make decisions in a premeditated way without fear a different, inner self will disapprove of my choices. Unlike neurotypicals like you, I don't wage interior battles between morality and personal desire when faced with a choice.*
>
> *– Nashville Kitty*
> *69 Shades of Nashville: Sociopathic Sex Southern Style*

Sociopaths have a lack of guilt or remorse. They are incapable of feeling these emotions, because they have no conscience. Unlike most of us, they do not have that little voice urging them to do what is right and moral.

GUILTLESS

For empathetic people, guilt is a given. Even when we are doing the right thing, we still worry if we have done enough. There are whole books written about extreme examples of people consumed with guilt when there is no necessity for it. Because these people feel guilty, they are frequently afraid to say, "No," and often are terrified that people will think they are selfish and insensitive.

Sociopaths have the opposite problem. It is possible that some of them may have a passing sense of "I should feel guilty," perhaps a twinge of guilt, but this vague feeling is quickly dismissed. Since it doesn't come up again for them, they are much more likely to fake guilt than to actually experience it.

Ironically, these same people love to make their victims feel guilty. It is a game for them and a rich source of power that can be used for manipulation. Sociopaths use our guilt against us. Each time they induce these feelings in others, it serves as a useful lesson on how to fake realistic guilt.

Lies*

*applies to sociopaths, psychopaths, and sexopaths

> The truth is a very tricky thing. As I have already mentioned, I am a masterful liar. I lie to cover my lies. Lying is a sociopath's primary weapon, and it comes as easily as breathing. Artful lies are a necessity to convince all the neurotypicals of the world I am one of them—whether it is to siphon a few extra bucks from the billing accounts of some clueless physicians or to ensnare a drooling puppy to serve me. Luckily, sociopaths are not limited by typical physiology and can even beat a polygraph machine. There is no tell-tale increase in heart rate or perspiration or change in blood pressure. We are cool as cucumbers as we weave our webs of deceit, knowing we are the most skilled spiders out there.
>
> – Nashville Kitty
> 69 Shades of Nashville: Sociopathic Sex Southern Style

Sociopaths are pathological liars who often tell lies just because they can. Lying is their weapon of choice. Part of their boredom prevention is seeing just how far they can trick some unassuming victim. How much can they get us to believe? Lying is fun for them, so they lie frequently for no apparent reason, just to see if they can get someone to fall for their falsehoods. In a relationship, intimate details contradict each other—the pillow talk doesn't add up.

Empathetic people feel an instinctive need to tell the truth. It is so much a part of our human nature that lying causes physiologic changes in our bodies including increased heart rate, sweating, and blood pressure fluctuations no matter how hard we try to suppress these reactions. Sociopaths don't have that problem and lie as easily as they breathe.

When sociopaths tell the truth, it is only because the truth happens to support their current agenda. Perhaps they know that you already know the truth of a situation so they are trying to portray themselves as a truthful person. Often it is easiest to hide a lie amongst multiple truths—just slip a lie in to see if anyone notices.

You may wonder why sociopaths go to all this trouble. It's not trouble for them—it is simply how they operate to prevent boredom and manipulate others. They love to see people react, to make them jump, and know that they caused that reaction. It is all part of the game. There is often no connection between what they are saying and reality. The lies do, however, support their underlying agenda.

When do normal people lie? Generally, when they are afraid of the consequences of the truth. At the same time, there is the conflicting urge to tell the truth which results in intense feelings of guilt. The sociopath does not have these reactions. With no fear or guilt, they experience a thrill from lying. It is "game on."

When caught in a lie, the sociopath will just offer more lies to cover up the first one. If that doesn't work, they will deny saying the first lie at all. They will say things to cover up the lie that are easily proven false in this modern age of the internet and fact checking, but they will insist that because they are saying it, it should be taken as fact. It is true because they say it is. If you disagree with them, you are an enemy, a traitor and must be out to get them.

FINGERS CROSSED

LIES DON'T COUNT

Infidelity*
*applies to sexopaths

ChainReaction
I thought your marriage was going great?

NashvilleKitty
It is. But to save it from an inevitable future
destruction caused by boredom and predictability,
it's imperative I'm able to have many, many affairs.
In fact, the more affairs I have, I imagine the happier
my husband's life will be.

ChainReaction
Happy wife, happy life.

NashvilleKitty
Exactly.

—69 Shades of Nashville: Sociopathic Sex Southern Style

CHEATERS'
CHECKLIST

1. Deny, Deny,
   Deny
2. Secret Phone
3. Secret P.O.Box
4. Secret bank
   account
5. Secret credit
   card

Sexopaths often have more than one relationship simultaneously, usually juggling these relationships using deception. Eventually, they use the technique of gaslighting (manipulating with psychological tactics to make someone question his/her own sanity), making their partner feel as if they are insane or paranoid for suspecting the truth. Sexopaths make you feel crazy for trusting your own eyes and for not believing their lies.

Infidelity is often the result with sexopaths who lack the ability to feel empathetic love but have a high sex drive. While an empathetic person who has a high sex drive may have the urge to seduce numerous people, hopefully, this individual will learn that seducing people has consequences: feelings get hurt, inconsolable jealousies arise, lessons are learned.

Without empathy, sexual conquest has no bounds or limits. There is never "too much" or a sense of "wrong" associated with the pursuit of pleasure. Sexopaths cannot be convinced that they are the cause of someone else's pain. If it felt good to them, how can their victim possibly call "foul?" And for sexopaths, they simply don't care anyway.

Manipulative*
*applies to sociopaths, psychopaths, and sexopaths

> Gone with the Wind is my favorite book and movie of all time—think of me as Scarlett. I live here on my very own Tara plantation, with suitors galore, and I manipulate the world around me to get what I want.
>
> – Nashville Kitty
> 69 Shades of Nashville: Sociopathic Sex Southern Style

To sociopaths, the world is a game and the rest of us are merely pawns to be manipulated. Everything is seen as a way to further their personal gain. Frequently, they play for your pity. Sociopaths love to obtain your sympathy as it makes you more vulnerable to manipulation.

Like an artist who uses many different sized brushes, shapes, and colors, their art of manipulation has countless tools. The more intelligent the sociopath, the more skilled they become in their manipulative art. Elements of personal interaction, which empathetic people take for granted, are sociopaths' weapons of manipulation.

ART OF MANIPULATION

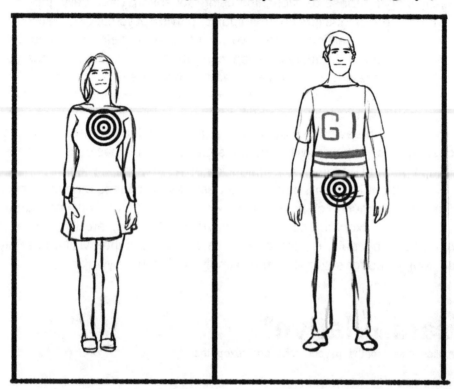

It is not uncommon when dealing with sociopaths for anything and everything that you experience in your interaction with them to be turned to benefit their agenda in the future—right down to details that would seem trivial to an empathetic person. An example in a workplace environment would be when a bored sociopath wants to gaslight a colleague.

During seemingly idle chit chat, the sociopath has catalogued all sorts of details about the colleague. The sociopath knows that the victim is allergic to roses and can't stand the smell of them because it brings back horrible childhood memories. She also knows that this colleague is very sensitive about her true age as she is the oldest in the office. This colleague also tends to be a "touch-me-not" type of person and, while she is very loving and well loved, she is not one to hug and prefers to keep a wide sense of personal space.

On the colleague's birthday, what does the sociopath do for no other reason than to entertain herself? She tells all the other people in the office that she would love to give this colleague a special birthday present. She convinces them that in order for it to be a surprise, they should pretend to have forgotten the colleague's birthday, so they can celebrate the following day. While everyone in the office goes about life as normal, all day long the colleague waits patiently for the routine 30 minutes of cake and ice cream to celebrate the occasion. Although this has occurred for many years past, this year everyone in the office ignores her.

As the day goes on, she starts looking dejected. She wonders if being the oldest in the office has made her no longer part of the group. Are they getting ready to fire her? Is she about to be forgotten? This is all the manipulation of the sociopath—it's the most fun she has had all month! With each passing hour, the sociopath delights in the increasing sadness of her colleague. Even the sociopath's body language is carefully controlled to affect more torture. She ignores her hurt colleague, making a point not to include her in any break time chat and avoids eye contact. On her birthday, the dejected colleague gets less attention rather than more. The sociopath is surprised when the colleague's eyes seem teary at the end of the day. The effect has been stronger than she anticipated—what a bonus!

The next day the fun continues as the sociopath brings the colleague, now surrounded by all her office mates, a dozen roses and then wishes her a happy birthday with a cake with the number "58" on it despite the fact that she is only 54. It isn't that the sociopath hates the colleague.

It isn't personal at all. She is just doing little malicious things out of boredom and the desire to win her game of manipulation. As the ring leader of this cruel birthday celebration, she demands that everybody give the colleague a big hug. She left no detail out, having spritzed herself with rose water perfume that day.

This is an example of manipulation in the workplace. Please check out *Snakes in Suits* for more fascinating information on this topic. Sociopaths use these and other manipulative techniques in romantic relationships as we will see later in this chapter.

Predatory Stare*

*applies to sociopaths, psychopaths, and sexopaths

> *He gawked at me, and I let him. I arched my back ever so slightly. Then, I tilted my sunglasses down just far enough for him to see the icy blue sparklers I used for eyes. Some puppies are off put by my predatory stare but others chose to focus on their own reflection. To each his own—I let them see whatever they wanted inside them.*
>
> *— Nashville Kitty*
> *69 Shades of Nashville: Sociopathic Sex Southern Style*

In the animal kingdom the attack of a predator always begins with the predatory stare. This is how the aggressor focuses its entire attention and efforts upon its prey. In similar fashion, sociopaths often stare in a way empathetic people don't.

For most people, eye contact is a means to increase a sense of empathy. We are literally trying to see through another's eyes. We open our eyes and through them express our understanding and trust. We remember the loving gaze of someone in our lives, a gaze that says "this person loves me and feels what I feel. This person is here with me. I feel oneness with this person."

For the sociopath however, this stare, this intense penetrating gazing of the eyes, acts almost as a piercing into the other person's soul. It can be mesmerizing, almost hypnotic. This is the hunter wanting to know the prey's weaknesses, trying to find the vulnerabilities which will advance the sociopath's agenda.

An unaware person might mistake the intensity of this look as a form of flattering attention, especially if done in a romantic setting. Some more sensitive people will sense the lack of caring in the stare and will instinctively feel ill at ease, even "creeped out" as it makes their skin crawl.

The empathetic person will occasionally have a searching, piercing gaze when trying to understand someone. Perhaps, at moments, the stare is more curious than loving but staring is not a typical human behavior. As in the story of Chloe and Larry, sociopaths regard people this way frequently. It has sometimes been described as undressing someone with their eyes. It is a physical clue that you may be dealing with a sociopath, so do not be afraid to discuss the predatory stare with others.

PREDATORY STARE

Sexopath Love Cycle*
*applies to sexopaths

As a sexopath, I don't need companionship the way you do, dear reader. I make myself plenty happy by leveraging peripheral acquaintances to get what I want. I don't have time for clutter. The only impetus for any relationship I keep is if it proved valuable or it gave me real, measurable pleasure. Dropping anyone who does not offer me something useful like incredible sex or a large checkbook is a given. I am like those insane minimalist organizers. Everything—and everyone—that doesn't offer pleasure or purpose gets donated to the local thrift shop. Sentimentality does not exist in my mind.

– Nashville Kitty
69 Shades of Nashville: Sociopathic Sex Southern Style

As exhibited in Chloe and Larry's story, the sexopath love stages are 1. Idealize 2. Devalue 3. Discard. Stage 1 incorporates "Love Bombing," in which the romance seems too good to be true. Victims are encouraged to believe they have found the perfect soul mate while sexopaths mirror back to you exactly what you want to see and hear. It is an act. Sexopaths are masters of disguise and will don the perfect mask tailored to your preferences. Sexopaths are charming, making victims feel like they are perfect and wonderful, while they love bomb them with texts, calls, letters, gifts, and attention. The goal is to inundate victims, so that they can't catch their breath, accurately evaluate things, and determine their own feelings. This stage is very intense, with the sexopath being increasingly impatient to move the relationship forward toward sex, commitment, even an announcement of devotion and love.

Once victims are hooked, then the Devalue stage starts—flickering between hot-and-cold, sometimes very sweet but then incredibly cruel. This keeps victims engaged with a desperate longing for the first stage of faked devotion to return. Sexopaths deliberately pick victims apart, causing self-doubt in the most vulnerable areas. By destroying self-esteem, victims question their value. Frequently, the goal is to isolate victims from friends and families, a common pattern in domestic abuse cases. Sexopaths no

SEXOPATH LOVE CYCLE

IDEALIZE   DEVALUE   DISCARD

longer idealize their victims and have started to get bored—their worst nightmare. Since nothing is ever a sexopath's fault according to sexopaths, their boredom must be the victims' fault. The sexopath blames the victim, because the sexopath is no longer infatuated—although the intent to destroy the victim may have been there from the outset. Typically, sexopaths pick those with the most empathy as this type person has what the sexopath lacks and is thus a worthy target to bring down. The hot-and-cold behavior is clinically called "intermittent reinforcement" and places victims on an emotional rollercoaster. Invariably, victims keep holding on for glimpses of their soul mate to return.

Once the hot-and-cold stage ends, sexopaths have complete contempt and disgust for their victims and can be vicious and vindictive. If the victim decides to leave first, the cycle may start over as the sexopath tries to regain control. Again, this is particularly common in domestic violence relationships with the cycle of love bombing that eventually degenerates to repeated violent episodes. Stalkers who are rejected by potential victims are often sexopaths.

Before the final stage 3, Discard, sexopaths will always claim to be dissatisfied with their partners, no matter what actions the partner takes to try to please, it is never good enough. If they do bend themselves into the perfect pretzel—sexopaths will simply declare that they like their pretzels straight and their victims should know that already. After taking what they wanted from you, sexopaths will discard you like a piece of trash without the slightest bit of guilt or remorse in order to find someone else for their next diabolical game. Often you will be left wondering, "What just happened?" You were conned by a sexopath. *Psychopath Free* by Jackson MacKenzie is an excellent book and website for additional information on this type of abusive relationship.

Empathy Lacking*
*applies to sociopaths, psychopaths, and sexopaths

What you should know up front is that sociopaths are an entirely different breed of humans. PET scans reveal our brains work differently—better, I would venture to say—as we do not suffer from many of the typical emotions that plague the rest of humanity, such as empathy, guilt, or remorse.

– Nashville Kitty
69 Shades of Nashville: Sociopathic Sex Southern Style

Since sociopaths lack empathy, they cannot experience what other people feel. They are able to understand what another person feels, they just don't have the emotional response—they can't actually *feel* it. Often, they are callous and cold and do not react as expected in many situations that would have resulted in an emotional response in an empathetic person. Because certain reactions are expected, sociopaths fake emotions.

Empathy is more than just a feeling. It is a phenomenon that is needed for love itself and is part of the indescribable beauty of human existence. For most people, empathy is more than instinctual, it is something they can observe happening within themselves. They know when they have it, and they are keenly aware in moments when they do not.

With sociopaths, trying to explain empathy or love to them is like trying to explain colors to someone who has been blind since birth. Since they have never experienced it, they have no reference point. They simply don't comprehend what they are missing. Ms. M.E. Thomas—a self-proclaimed sociopath who follows a religious set of ethics resulting in her being a very functional and productive member of society (check out her book *Confessions of a Sociopath: Hiding in Plain Sight* for a fascinating read)—believes even as a sociopath, she experiences love. However, in her very description, it is clear that she is not talking about the empathetic love described in art, literature, and movies throughout the ages. I would not go so far as to say what she experiences is not a *type* of love but gathering "as much information as possible about every aspect of the person's life in order to more closely resemble their ideal mate" is NOT what the rest of us are talking about when we talk about love. Empathetic love involves a soul connection—sociopaths can't do that.

Empathetic people can choose to become more empathetic by paying attention to adverse circumstances, then considering empathy intellectually and amplifying it in their lives. Thus, we can become better at being empathetic. It is the natural progression of wisdom as we live and grow older. Of all the things sociopaths experience in their existence, emotional empathy is the weakest and most fleeting of all their experiences.

EMPATHY LACKING

Breaks the Law/Rules*

*applies to sociopaths, psychopaths, and sexopaths

Order and rules are very important in the video game of life, and I believe in following the rules if they suit me. If not, I simply change them. Changing rules is how we sociopaths move society forward.

– Nashville Kitty
69 Shades of Nashville: Sociopathic Sex Southern Style

Since sociopaths do not feel that rules apply to them, they often participate in criminal behavior. Sometimes they get caught and end up in jail, resulting in a higher percentage of sociopathic (especially psychopathic) people being found in prisons. Most sociopaths (including psychopaths), however, are not in jail, but among us. There is some thought that socioeconomic standing may affect whether a sociopath ends up in jail since those with more money and power are better able to maneuver and escape incarceration. Expensive lawyers have been known to plea bargain many a wealthy sociopath out of prison time.

Empathetic people have an innate sense that individuals in society as a whole benefit from rules. They may argue about which rules are good and which are bad but believe it is necessary to both create and follow society's restrictions. To sociopaths, rules are regarded in a much different manner. Rules for them are merely the reasons they give themselves for their actions. It seems logical to them to change the rules to suit their agenda. By this logic, they are not breaking the rules since they have already changed them. They are simply following the new rules they have created for their personal benefit. It could be argued that they don't understand the concept of rules as most people do. In fact, they frequently will brag about breaking rules, often not hiding their tendency to change the rules in an instant.

Egotistical*
*applies to sociopaths, psychopaths, and sexopaths

> I got to the bedroom and slipped out of my clothes. I looked at myself in our big, floor-to-ceiling mirror. All modesty aside—sociopaths are sometimes accused of being narcissistic, but it is simply appreciating our own self-worth—I am quite attractive in a uniquely Nashvillian way. I have straightened, bleached-blonde hair, artificially tanned skin, and piercing ice blue eyes. I used them to gaze at my dainty five-foot-two, 105-pound frame while cupping my man-made—and men-approved—D cups. My abs and buns were tight and a pleasure to behold. I worked out and ate right, remembering what my daddy always said: "If you believe you're hot, so will they."

> – Nashville Kitty
> 69 Shades of Nashville: Sociopathic Sex Southern Style

"Narcissistic, delusions of grandeur, grandiose sense of self" often

HOW MANY SOCIOPATHS DOES IT TAKE TO CHANGE A LIGHT BULB?

Just one – the world revolves around me!

EGOTISTICAL

describes sociopaths' high opinion of themselves. Although found within the Narcissistic Personality Disorder, it is also part of the sociopathic makeup and is often the easiest way to identify them (especially the common hypochondria or self-absorbed belief that they have all sorts of physical diseases and bogus health problems, a trait common in sociopaths).

All sociopaths are narcissists but not all narcissists are sociopaths (the difference is determined by whether the person has empathy and a conscience).

According to the sociopathic perspective, they are special and should be regarded as such. One strong clue to the presence of sociopaths is one minute they are bragging about how great they are, then, when they are caught in compromising positions, they turn the tables to make it somehow someone else's fault or the fault of circumstances. Suddenly, they are the victims, trying to make their audience feel sorry for them and give them another chance. After the crisis, they are back to believing they are omnipotent. To add to their grandeur, sociopaths and sexopaths may brag about numerous past sexual conquests, featuring themselves as the most desirable and indomitable lovers.

Whereas empathetic people will sacrifice themselves for the benefit of other people, even total strangers, sociopaths feel no such urge. The only wants and needs that influence their actions are their own. It is all about the self, and they can't see self as part of the larger group. It is all about them. They are the center of the universe—and everybody should know that already!

Empathetic people identify themselves as not only individuals but also as members of family, church, community, and the human race. Identity includes more than just the self. Sociopaths do not experience this sense of expanded self. If asked "Who are you?" their only answer would be "I am me" and nothing more.

Hollow Emotions*
*applies to sociopaths, psychopaths, and sexopaths

> We do not experience emotions or attachments the same way you do. Some unenlightened scientists have described the sociopath as having the empathy of a five-year-old, whereas psychopaths have none. However, a more accurate explanation is that our emotions can be turned on and off like a light switch depending on what is most convenient for us. Despite debate on the actual percentage of sociopaths—we are not plentiful, but neither are we rare—we recognize each other and can form alliances for mutual benefit; however, we will then betray one another without a second thought if a better opportunity presents itself.
>
> – *Nashville Kitty*
> *69 Shades of Nashville: Sociopathic Sex Southern Style*

Sociopaths are cold, callous, with no fear, love, or worry beyond themselves. Sociopaths as young children, show a lack of complexity in their emotions at an early age. Their lack of empathy/caring about other people may be evident to parents and especially children as bullying behavior. Although they may exhibit momentary happiness or anger, they lack other emotions most children experience by age 8. Sociopaths may have some base emotions, but their emotions tend to be all or nothing.

In life, sociopaths learn to fake emotions in order to manipulate people and to fit in. There is a degree of complexity to this acting which can be difficult to comprehend. For sociopaths, emotions are purely an act to be tirelessly performed. It is not possible to always be perfect in their pretense; however, some are exceptionally good at it. They can even trick psychological experts. A recommendation from M.E. Thomas as to how to beat a sociopath, is to feed the sociopath false information. Remember that sociopaths have no empathy, so they are dependent on your verbal and facial cues to figure out what you feel and expect. If you provide no or misleading information, the sociopath does not know how to manipulate you—not that I am advising you to become a lying hypocrite to play games with sociopaths, because stooping to their level is bound to turn out poorly for you—but it is interesting to monitor a sociopath who is unable to sort out your verbal and nonverbal cues.

Sociopaths regard the inability of empathetic people to turn off emotions as a sign of weakness. Since they despise true emotions, they intellectually condemn people who can't turn emotions off at will.

Irresponsible*
*applies to sociopaths, psychopaths, and sexopaths

> *I did well enough in college to easily get into medical school, but when I saw the bags under the eyes of the medical students on campus, I knew it wasn't the life for me. I don't care enough about other people to waste my time saving their lives. Science stimulates me only to the extent that I know how to use biological tricks in bed and how to sharpen my psychological edge.*
>
> *– Nashville Kitty*
> *69 Shades of Nashville: Sociopathic Sex Southern Style*

Sociopaths love to take the credit but detest doing the work. They often live a parasitic lifestyle by living off others or getting others to do their work for them while they bask in the glory. Frequently unreliable, they don't show up when required. Despite their bragging, they are often sloppy and make mistakes.

The actions of sociopaths to an empathetic person can seem consistently irresponsible and reckless. At the same time, sociopaths are unaware of their own weakness and deluded about their superiority, so they often take foolish risks. This is one of the more unexplained aspects of sociopaths. They do not seem to be capable of comprehending their own mortality and exhibit no fear. Even more alarming, since they don't care about their own deaths, they also show an inability to be responsible for the life, safety, and well-being of other people. Since they do things without considering the consequences to themselves or others, they may be very poor financial planners and may gamble money in a very reckless way. Sometimes this turns out well, but other times, it is a disaster. This is part of their lack of impulse control. Even when they can fake emotions such as empathy, love, and caring, they generally cannot hide their lack of responsibility so this is a trait you can spot. Even the highly intelligent and well-hidden sociopath demonstrates this characteristic at times.

Not Me*

*applies to sociopaths, psychopaths, and sexopaths

> If I found the right sugar daddy, maybe I could leverage his wealth to find more ripe and exotic fruit. That's it! It's not the kitty that's the problem—it's Nashville!
>
> – Nashville Kitty
> 69 Shades of Nashville: Sociopathic Sex Southern Style

To sociopaths, nothing is ever their fault—how could it be when they are perfect in every way? They blame others or circumstances for all of their problems, utilizing the victim role whenever it is to their advantage to do so.

Whenever starting new relationships, it is wise to ask about your potential partner's old relationships and how they ended. For sociopaths, the past partners were always the ones to blame. Sociopaths may even brag about getting even, boasting about waiting years to exact revenge so the former partner wouldn't anticipate it. All ex-lovers will be vilified as it was always the sociopath's misfortune to be involved with someone who was so unworthy of affection. The ex-'s are all crazy, jealous, and bipolar. Since they never accept blame, the responsibility for a relationship's end is never their fault. They blame others, circumstances, or a malevolent fate.

Empathetic people can grow and mature, acknowledging that they have done regrettable things and even that they are likely to do more regrettable things in the future. We understand that all people do something wrong at times and that it may be necessary to make amends and apologize. This concept is completely missing to sociopaths who never accept blame in any sincere way. Although they might at times pretend to be sorry as part of a greater goal, inside they are laughing at anyone who believes their remorseful charade. For sociopaths, an important skill in the manipulative arts that can enable them to get what they want in life is to blame other people. Not only does it provide the obvious escape from their own retribution, it is also a useful tool to torment other people by placing blame that is not deserved. Through their manipulative actions, they hope that another group of people will turn and persecute their innocent victims.

Danger Seekers*

*applies to sociopaths, psychopaths, and sexopaths

Obviously, I didn't want to get caught. No one wants to get caught. The thrill-seeking inherent in adultery is something that draws us sociopaths to the sport. Part of the allure is that you might get caught, even though the neurotypicals will usually be the ones taking the fall.

— *Nashville Kitty*
69 Shades of Nashville: Sociopathic Sex Southern Style

Sociopaths have decreased function in their brains where impulse control is found, making them impulsive and prone to reckless behavior. They will put themselves and others in danger without regard to the potential consequences. They are missing a sense of fear and awareness of safety. In addition, they are thrill seekers because they hate to be bored. Since merely existing is a terrible boredom to them, they seek out experiences which excite them physically and stimulate their minds at the same time. Since they have no fear of death, they naturally gravitate towards dangerous activities.

PLAYING WITH EXPLOSIVES

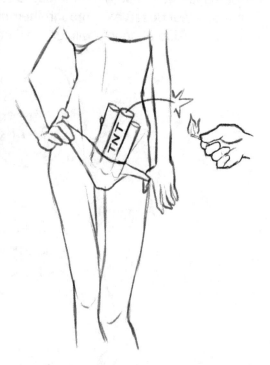

For example, one notable sociopath, M.E. Thomas, won't allow herself to use knives because she knows she has no safety awareness and got tired of ending up at the Emergency Department after cutting herself again and again. As a highly intelligent individual, she acknowledges the situation and removes possible temptation.

WHAT COULD GO WRONG?!!

While many empathetic people might engage in dangerous behavior, they contemplate the risks involved. Sociopaths, on the other hand, will be too busy basking in the exhilaration of declaring themselves invincible to deal with the consequences of danger. They might brag about something being dangerous and how afraid they were but, despite their words, they are faking being scared. Their mannerisms do not match their words.

As anyone who has known a teenage driver can attest, risk calculation is something that people get better at as they get older. Since they lack fear of death and injury, sociopaths are not likely to be better at risk calculation unless there is some other motivation. There is some evidence that sociopathic traits (particularly impulsivity and aggressive behavior—traits that can lead to imprisonment) may lessen after age 40 (perhaps as a result of decreased testosterone), but this is still to be decisively determined.

Targeting Next Sexual Encounter*

*applies to sexopaths

> *What hadn't dawned on me until late in my high school career was expanding my search for trainable puppies to other schools. Why restrict yourself to a single dog breeder when there are so many available kennels out there?*
>
> *– Nashville Kitty*
> *69 Shades of Nashville: Sociopathic Sex Southern Style*

Sexopaths are constantly on the prowl for their next sexual encounter and victim. Some are obsessed with sex and plan their lives around the next sexual adventure. Sex becomes a much higher priority than other responsibilities, so much so that they let family and work responsibilities lapse in order to get their next sexual fix.

Whenever sexopaths meet a potential victim, they go through an evaluation of possible weaknesses and vulnerabilities that effectively can be manipulated. While empathetic people when meeting someone tend to find mutual ground or are worried about how the other person is perceiving them, sexopaths are unconcerned about anything except their personal agenda.

MEAT AND GREET

There are many factors which contribute to the compulsive behavior of sexopaths who are always looking for the next person to fall under their spell. It is almost incomprehensible to empathetic people that sexopaths are always looking for victims. It is even more difficult to conceive that after the first victim falls, the sexopath is already looking for someone else.

Head Honcho*
*applies to sociopaths, psychopaths, and sexopaths

> *History is made by people willing to use the backs of hunched over, guilty souls as a staircase to power.*
>
> *– Nashville Kitty*
> *69 Shades of Nashville: Sociopathic Sex Southern Style*

In an ideal world, a position of power comes with the responsibility of behaving for the common good. Unfortunately, positions of power often are occupied by sociopaths. Although anyone in a position of power should earn the trust of subordinates—after all, they are suspect just because they have obtained a position of power—there are frequent cases of abuse. Is this person a sexopath who uses a position of power to coerce subordinates for sexual favors and to advance sexual gratification? Is a position of power a means for additional control over subordinates for personal gain?

Being seen as a leader or revered in positions of power are places toward which sociopaths naturally gravitate. In fact, they never stop attempting to move up the ladder of any organization when there exists a position above them. How high they rise and how powerful they become in the organization is generally a function of their intelligence, socioeconomic background, and luck in life. Lesser intelligent sociopaths might do well to be the pastor of a church in a rural town of 200 people. In contrast, the most successful intelligent sociopaths will gravitate to ultimate positions of power such as heads of state and CEO's of international organizations.

Ironically, because sociopaths are not burdened with caring for others, they are left with more time and mental energy to rise above more empathetic people. They don't pursue positions of power because they are responsible, but rather from a desire for power for its own sake. Empathetic people are often reluctant to take on the extra duties and responsibilities necessitated by a position of power but sacrifice themselves because they care so much about a task or duty. In contrast, consider the CEO who plays golf every day while leaving necessary decisions to his subordinates. If those decisions are wrong, it is never his fault.

STAIRCASE TO POWER

Expressional Inconsistencies*

*applies to sociopaths, psychopaths, and sexopaths

> *While I don't choose to feel emotions, I am among the best at pretending I do.*
>
> *– Nashville Kitty*
> *69 Shades of Nashville: Sociopathic Sex Southern Style*

Because sociopaths are incapable of empathy, they must act by donning a mask to fit into society and to pick up on social cues from those around them. This provides the opportunity for empathetic people to glimpse behind the mask by monitoring for micro-inflections that are lacking or revealed in social situations.

INSIDE — I'm a weed whacker!

OUTSIDE — I'm Southern sweet With a killer smile

When watching a sociopath, one thing that often will be noticeably absent are tiny micro-inflections in the face. Micro-inflections are little muscle twitches of the face that denote a person's first emotional response. They only last seconds and are frequently missed. Evident in empathetic people is the subtle rise of the eyebrows when empathy is felt as well as a softening of the eyes and perhaps a slight opening of the mouth. Initially, the outward signs of someone's heartstrings being tugged will be absent in the sociopath. It doesn't matter how inspiring or empathy-inducing the story is, there will a momentary lack of expression and the sociopath will not be able to keep their mask perfectly identical to the first reactions of an empathetic person. It takes a few seconds for the sociopath to realize that a look of empathy is expected and then, ironically, the sociopath will often over do the response. Observing the reaction at the right moment can provide a good indication that a sociopath is present.

When a sociopath experiences anger (one of the few emotions sociopaths do experience deeply), the micro-inflections are visible at the moment of initial emotion. The movements are very subtle, but their facial expression changes for a split second before the sociopath regains control. Look for when anger micro-inflections in the facial expressions that quickly disappear when the sociopath reapplies the mask. Other subtler emotions remain lacking. Even when sociopaths describe an act of violence, there will be a lack of empathy in the storytelling. Sometimes they are monotone in their delivery. Compare this with the unconscious facial changes that are often signatures of the empathetic soul. It is in the unrehearsed moments that you can spot sociopaths.

To the observant person, it is possible to catch sociopaths when they try to understand when they are supposed to feel guilty. Empathetic people will show micro-inflections with such body language as eyes popping open, an instinctive reaction even before there is conscious awareness that they feel guilt. Sociopaths don't have the physical reaction first. They can be happy and smiling until, all of a sudden, they need to pretend that they feel guilty. The spread of the response may depend on the sociopath's degree of intelligence and forethought, making some sociopaths easier to spot than others. Some may just be naturally better actors than others, depending on the individual's abilities. No matter how intelligent the sociopath and no matter how focused they are on faking emotion, they simply lack the micro-inflections that empathetic people have for caring, sadness, remorse, and love.

Magnetism*

*applies to sociopaths, psychopaths, and sexopaths

> *I left my place at the grill, disappointing the half-dozen men*
> *that had found it the most interesting place to be, so long as I*
> *was there.*

> *– Nashville Kitty*
> *69 Shades of Nashville: Sociopathic Sex Southern Style*

Sociopaths are known for their superficial charm; they can sell ice to an Eskimo and bring a tear to a glass eye. In addition, they have the uncanny ability to mirror back exactly what their victims want to see. They can appear to be the perfect soul mate while changing their personality as often as they change their clothes.

The magnetism of sociopaths is not something clearly understood. Why do empathetic people feel so drawn, captivated, and subservient to them? Although it seems almost magical and supernatural at times, someday science may provide a better understanding of this mechanism.

Even highly intelligent people who can write and converse extensively about sociopaths are not immune to the power of their charm. For individuals who really don't understand sociopaths exist, they are easy and defenseless victims when sociopaths choose to focus upon them. History is replete with examples of leaders who have all the traits of sociopaths and who galvanize whole countries into doing their bidding. Mussolini during World War II, Stalin in U.S.S.R., Cambodian dictator Pol Pot, and Saddam Hussein may be examples of this type of leader.

On a more individual level, it is always advisable to monitor your own responses to other people. When you are swept away by someone's charm, it is wise to ask, "Could this person be a sociopath? Am I being manipulated? Am I being fooled by false flattery and unrealistic promises? Why am I drawn to this person?"

Anger*
*applies to sociopaths, psychopaths, and sexopaths

How dare he! How dare this groveling little geek, whom I gifted with even a glimpse of my body, much less a touch of it, overstep his boundaries and try to give me advice? And advice about my family? My life. How dare he!

– Nashville Kitty
69 Shades of Nashville: Sociopathic Sex Southern Style

Although sociopaths experience very few true, sincere emotions, anger and contempt are two of them. They can be prone to fits of rage and violence. Since they can't always get their way, they can be observed having higher levels of anger with increased frequency.

This cannot be easily hidden from an empathetic person and will often seem both childish and excessive. When looking for clues of a potential sociopath, empathetic people should be advised to be aware of this abnormal anger when it is visible, and when it obviously is being suppressed. Sociopaths often use anger to shift blame when confronted with wrongdoing. Oddly, the anger fit often ends suddenly, and the sociopath will act like everything is back to normal. Frequently, empathetic people will walk on eggshells around the sociopath, fearing the next outburst of anger.

When you get angry, count to ten...

When you get to seven, throw a punch

No one expects that!

Sex Addiction*

*applies to sexopaths

I'm not a monster. I just enjoy sex. It is neck and neck with manipulation as my favorite hobby of choice. I'm obsessed with sex the same way most people are devoted to perfectly innocent pastimes like sports, movies, and prayer. My obsession is no more perverted than worshipping devotees at a Sunday service. If anything, mine makes more sense because it's not imaginary. It's visceral. It's real. It's biology.

– Nashville Kitty
69 Shades of Nashville: Sociopathic Sex Southern Style

Some sexopaths are selfish lovers, only caring about pleasing the other person as far as it can benefit themselves. Their goals are personal benefit by taking control and adding another notch to their belts. Once they have experienced their personal sexual gratification, they are on to the next conquest. This game has been won, and it is time to go to the next one.

On the other hand, some sexopaths derive pleasure from making another person lose control. They desire the adoration of being "the best lover ever" as they take charge in passionate lovemaking in order to release the addictive neurotransmitters of orgasm. Sex is a means of control.

Often sexopaths have had over 100 partners, boasting there are "too many to remember." Ironically, it is not uncommon that sexopaths do not even orgasm. Since the game is more about the conquest and control than actual sexual release, orgasm can be irrelevant. They will often have sex with random strangers in risky locations. In a relationship, they expect lovers to have sex when, where, and how often they want.

Sexopaths are prone to all sorts of addictions, sex being one of them. Having multiple addictions is common. Not all sex addicts are sexopaths but sex addiction can be a quick and sure sign of a sexopath who might have otherwise remained well hidden.

Sex addiction isn't how much or how often the person likes sex. Rather, it is the motivation behind the sex drive. For sexopaths, sex addiction is frequently identified by the lack of concern for the person who is the focus of their desire. Whereas with empathetic people, sex can bring people closer together and be the ultimate act of intimacy, for sexopaths, there is a total absence of this desire. Although it might take careful attention to detect this behavior, most victims eventually perceive the resulting lies and insincerity.

Although sexopaths can at first seem to be gracious and loving sex partners, they tend to forget to extend the charade when bragging of former lovers. How they speak of other people can be more telling than how they are treating their current victims. One of the hardest things for sexopaths to understand is how incredibly outrageous their actions can be. For example, this could be someone who arranges sex trysts online while a partner is sleeping in the next room, then the next day has another tryst with a different person during lunch. The partner, who upon discovering clues of the cheating, doubts the reality of the cheating because the obvious truth is so unbelievable.

Sexopaths will be at their weakest if ever they fail to control the manipulation or plan a careful deception that falters. Ironically, this weakness will be a result of an intense drive for sexual gratification that makes both empathetic people and sexopaths reckless and impulsive.

I don't suffer from a sex addiction. Really, I quite enjoy it!

SEX ADDICTION

Kill for Power & Control*

*applies to sociopaths, psychopaths, and sexopaths

I am a sociopath—I need control and power like plants need water and sunlight. Without either of those things, I felt like I was going to die.

– Nashville Kitty
69 Shades of Nashville: Sociopathic Sex Southern Style

Power and control are two of the favorite highs most sought by sociopaths. They tend to use "kill" often in their vocabulary—a clue that a sociopath is present. Since everything is a game and they want to win at all costs, the idea of "killing" is a logical extension, if unrealistic.

Even if "killing" is not involved, sociopaths carry grudges. They are very vengeful and often will brag about obtaining revenge. Although homicidal thoughts and feelings are certainly not exclusive to sociopaths, what is different is that empathetic people instinctively feel an intense sense of wrong about killing. It is this moral voice that calms empathetic people down and prevents anger from becoming action. Lacking an internal moral compass, sociopaths have no instinctive counter reaction to the thought of taking life. For sociopaths, the mechanism that prevents them from physically hurting or harming other people is one of practicality. Murder and violence would simply get in the way of their ultimate goals, not to mention all the unreasonable questions police detectives tend to ask.

Impulse control is even less higher up on The Sociopath Spectrum where the psychopaths live. Still, the tendency for sociopaths to be imperfect in their façade means that they use phrases involving killing, violence, and angry retribution noticeably more than empathetic people.

In addition, sociopaths can be observed using violent language as they talk about their conquests, whether work related or merely social. The pattern is that they want to win and get their way at all costs even if violence is necessary. Sociopaths don't believe in win-win negotiation. If ever they find themselves to be on the losing side, they will fixate on revenge. Since sociopaths can hold a grudge, they frequently feel revenge is often best served cold. They can wait years before attacking their victims. There are numerous cases where former victims have left their tormentors, remarried, and moved to far away locations only to be followed and murdered by their sociopathic ex-lovers years later.

Summary

Hopefully, this has clarified how to spot a sexopath, sociopath, or psychopath. It isn't easy and requires careful observation. You're unlikely to reach any conclusions from one encounter, but the first step to recognition is awareness, and this chapter should begin that process.

Aside from the scientific community's squeamishness when it comes to sex and its slowness when it comes to pressing social issues, the foremost reason sexopathy has remained an unnamed condition until now is because so few people can see it. The condition is incredibly challenging for the average person to recognize without proper tools. Identifying sexopathy is the essential first step in surviving in our current, sexopathic world and the spotting tool is a start.

Chapter 6: NashvilleKitty Exposed

Throughout this book, I've opened every chapter with an anecdote about sexopathic behavior. Although sexopathy has always existed in human society, we've become more aware of incidents of this type

behavior through news stories and the willingness of friends to share their experiences. The anecdotes are there to help you understand how sexopaths function. Using The Sexopathy Spotting Tool serves as a guideline to help you better identify and react to sexopathic behavior, but, like any tool, you have to put it into action if you plan to learn to recognize a sexopath.

As a prime example, it helps to look at the most in-depth story of sexopathy ever: NashvilleKitty. The anti-hero narrator of my novel *69 Shades of Nashville* revels in being a sexopath. Now, it's time to look at her behavior more closely. As with all NashvilleKitty examples used in this book, I will set up the references so you do not need to have read the novel first. However, getting inside the mind of an actual sexopath will help you understand how they truly think, so please feel free to enjoy *69 Shades of Nashville: Sociopathic Sex Southern Style* and analyze NashvilleKitty as a true sexopath.

Applying The Sexopath Spotting Tool to NashvilleKitty

Since it is a first-person novel, there are moments when NashvilleKitty is only speaking to herself internally. This obviously presents a problem to those of us trying to identify sexopathic behavior from an objective viewpoint. NashvilleKitty's analysis of herself is definitely skewed in her favor. Still, many of the internal moments NashvilleKitty describes can be instructive for how sexopathy functions. Since this truly is how she thinks, it can give hints to ways it manifests itself in our world. With that in mind, we'll see both internal and external examples of her behavior to help present a rounded picture of a sexopath. I will use the word "sexopath" to describe NashvilleKitty throughout this chapter as that is what she is. Whenever the word "sexopath" is used to represent NashvilleKitty, it also means "sociopath" as she is a sociopathic sex addict.

Guiltless

NashvilleKitty has no conscience. She does not experience guilt or remorse like the rest of us. There is no little voice in her head scolding her for her wrongdoings. Since she thinks only of fulfilling her desires, she never once considers how her actions could make others feel. She differs from empathetic people in that while empathetic people still have affairs, they would most likely have inner conflict, including guilt, over the morality of their decisions.

For example, when NashvilleKitty is deciding to take her newest conquest into the house she shares with her husband:

> *My mind immediately rushed to the basement. The place most suburban husbands turned into their man cave, I considered my kennel. I kept my affairs discreet but savored the opportunity to raise the stakes by bringing one of my puppies' home. I loved the idea of playing with them beneath the ground Hubby walked. Even when he was home, he almost never came down to the basement. It was my lair. Like any good kennel, I had enough toys to entertain a whole litter. I slowly slid open the patio door and beckoned LandscapeLover inside. It is time to taste his crop.*

Most people would feel guilty taking a new lover into the house shared with their spouse, but NashvilleKitty has no sense of remorse or twinge of conscience. In fact, she gets excited about doing the wrong thing. She delights in sleeping with her lovers under the ground Hubby walks.

Patti-cake,

Patti-cake,

Where's your man?

Making me come,

Fast as he can!

Lies

NashvilleKitty lies as easily as she breathes—and she is proud of it! Sexopaths are pathological liars who make up the craziest stories just to see if they can get you to believe them. They will tell lies simply because they are bored and lying is their form of entertainment. Read what NashvilleKitty has to say:

> *Being limited in their cognitive abilities, most neurotypicals will believe something fed to them multiple times. For example, I always told people I was incapable of lying if you look me in the eyes. That—of course—was a lie. I am an incredible liar, as all sociopaths are, but by telling people I can't lie they believe me when I do. I just love this trick!*

More intelligent sexopaths have mastered the art of the "technical truth" which is literally true while leading someone to an incorrect conclusion. NashvilleKitty goes on her first date using a cheaters' website called Aubrey Madeline. Before she meets her prospective new lover, she happened to talk to her younger sister Mindy who informed her that she had to cut off one of the guys she was dating. That little piece of information comes in handy when she receives a text from her husband and is put in a tricky position (and I'm not talking sexually):

> *I sat across from ItalianStallion, focusing on the way his eyebrows twitched every time he asked a question, like an antenna looking for a signal. He had begun his retort to my Q&A with inquires of his own. He was a deception novice, and I parried all his efforts as easily as his eyes were drawn to my chest. I felt my phone vibrate in my pocket, indicating an incoming text.*
>
> > *Hubby*
> > *Hey Honey! Where are you?*
>
> *I looked at the wilted lettuce on my plate, then up at ItalianStallion's face, those furry eyebrows twitching faster and faster as he spoke.*

<u>*Me*</u>
I'm at lunch.

I stopped typing and stared at his mouth. It was like an auctioneer calling the Kentucky Derby. I remembered my sister having to recently drown one of her pups—the quarterback—for talking too much and annoying her. She said he called too many plays, too fast. Now he had no one to hike him the ball. Speed had its time and place. It was a way of getting ahead of the curve on the track.

<u>*Me*</u>
My sister just broke up with her boyfriend.

I set my phone down and smiled, pretending to enjoy his nonsense and wondered whether the stereotype that the French are excellent lovers was true. My phone vibrated again, but I knew I didn't need to monitor it anymore. Everything would be fine on the home front, and I didn't have to tell a single lie. The statement was completely true. I was at lunch, and my sister did just break up with one of her many boyfriends. If Hubby incorrectly concluded I was at lunch with my sister, well then, that's on him. Truth is always a matter of perspective. The only thing to regret was my food order. I preferred a bloody steak to a flimsy salad.

I'm the queen of lies!

Clearly, NashvilleKitty qualifies as someone who tells half-truths (or technical truths) without too much trouble. It's clear she exhibits this sexopathic behavior. While most people would feel guilty, she relishes the subterfuge.

When caught in a lie, sexopaths will tell more lies to cover up previous lies and then expect you to believe the lies simply because they say so. If you question a sexopath's lies, an angry outburst may follow, somehow blaming you because you refuse to believe the lie being fed to you.

Sexopaths will also lie to themselves and will seem to believe their own lies in a delusional manner. NashvilleKitty is obsessed with convincing herself and everyone else that she is a sociopath and not a psychopath by claiming she is not violent—something that is not accurate when examining her words and actions. Ultimately, making this distinction is not important. She lies to herself to continue the pretty picture of superiority she chooses to believe about herself.

Infidelity

Sexopaths can have multiple relationships using deception. Because they lack the ability to feel guilt or remorse, sexopaths can lie freely to numerous lovers in order to obtain their own sexual satisfaction. Lacking a moral compass, sexopaths can actually rationalize that their actions are the best for everyone.

> *Being a self-aware sexopath with a taste for the risk and rewards of extramarital affairs is my big secret. Keeping that fact hidden adds to the danger of the game but also to the strength of our bond. Neurotypical society's opaque morals don't always agree. It would judge me with its small-minded morality. Just because I have the balls to do what they merely fantasize about, doesn't give people the right to deem me immoral and prevent me from getting what I want. Maybe you, reader, are on their side. What you probably aren't intelligent enough to understand is that if I didn't act on my desires, my house wouldn't be such a happy place. In fact, if I had spent my afternoon frustrated that I couldn't do what I wanted based on the rules society arbitrarily drew up*

*for me, maybe our home-cooked meal wouldn't be so peaceful.
If I were a neurotypical, maybe I'd let my emotions get the better
of me, and I'd take out my anger on Hubby by critiquing the way
he sometimes opens his mouth when he chews. Since I'm a
sexopath, I don't have to worry about my emotions boiling over. I
know better than to even put myself in such a stressful situation. I
just do what I want and don't worry about it.*

Her lack of conscience and inability to feel regret allows her to do what she wants and not worry about it. Most people would feel guilty for cheating on their spouse with multiple lovers, but not NashvilleKitty. As a self-serving sexopath, she enjoys manipulating anyone who crosses her path.

Manipulation

Manipulation is one of NashvilleKitty's favorite pastimes. Life is a game and people are simply pawns to be manipulated for her personal benefit. The desire to manipulate is present in every interaction she has with other people. Here is how she sets out to seduce Neighborhood Dad right in front of his wife and Hubby at the neighborhood potluck picnic.

Flirting is where it all begins. I can gather so much from a glance, a brief touch, or a chuckle. Naturally, as a calculating sexopath, I catalog every motion and emotion in my mind to develop a strategy for how to get what I want. Every seemingly innocent interaction is run through a highly sophisticated analysis as I deconstruct the path to successful completion. I enjoy the process as much as I do the endgame—sometimes more. The people in my life are pawns to tinker with on any game board of my choosing. Once I've collected enough data, I can write and rewrite the rules as I please. In this way, vulnerability in a neurotypical is as easy to spot as green mold on a light brown burger bun.

Enticing someone to cheat on a spouse is even more exciting when the spouse puts up a fight. I stood beside the barbecue asking Neighborhood Dad to detail his meat grilling technique for a solid thirty minutes before his model wife stepped in to meddle. When she finally came over to see what was burning, she didn't even notice how hopelessly lost he'd gotten himself in my cleavage. I tossed my angelic, shoulder-length blonde hair to the side, smiled, and agreed with her that men certainly cannot multitask.

"True," she said. "We're lucky if we can get them to do even one thing right!"

I almost started salivating as I pictured the one activity in which I hoped her husband excelled.

"Totally," I agreed. She and I had spoken previously a few times. I always make sure to be friendly to women first, whether or not I want to sleep with their husbands or boyfriends. If I can befriend them, I lower any suspicions. How could their friend ever sleep with their man?

"How are things with you two?" she asked, looking over at my husband, who was helping the other mothers portion out food for their kids.

"I mean, just look at the guy." I laid it on thick, and she ate it up. "He's my perfect angel."

I felt like a kid in the sandbox with all the toys to myself. A neurotypical housewife? A domesticated husband? Manipulating these two was going to be as easy as stuffing a bucket full of sand and turning it upside down to make my princess pleasure tower.

NashvilleKitty's manipulation involves presenting the proper mask for each of her intended targets while she casually collects information to be used for leverage in the future. She reveals very little about her true self but will present a well-crafted back story lie if needed.

Just gotta pull the right string!

THE HUBBY
PUPPET SHOW

Predatory Stare

The predatory stare is a huge clue when trying to spot a sexopath. When you see it and know what that unblinking stare means, it is unmistakable. NashvilleKitty uses her predatory stare to hypnotize her prey as she establishes her dominance with GeorgiaBulldog.

Keeping my eyes fixed on his, I glided gracefully toward him without any hesitation and grabbed his baby blue tie, just below the knot. With a provocative swish of my hips, I pulled him to attention while I straddled his lap. It was time he knew who wore the pants in this relationship.

Just as the rabbit freezes when caught in the eyes of a wolf, GeorgiaBulldog falls prey to the NashvilleKitty stare.

Sexopath Love Cycle

The sexopath love cycle is: Idealize, Devalue, Discard. NashvilleKitty's brief affair with Neighborhood Dad certainly follows this pattern.

Idealize: She has had her eye on Neighborhood Dad for some time and plans her means of attack and seduction. She uses flirting as well as her physical charms to lure him over to her house with the manufactured excuse of returning an empty dish she purposely left at the potluck picnic. Although considered demeaning to women in some circles, NashvilleKitty happily uses the appearance of her body to trap men.

Some people use commands like "Come" or "Heel" to lead their puppies to their side; I use the visual call of a well-rounded butt to bring my prospective lovers to my kennel at a fast pace.

Devalue: After sex on the carpet, empathetic Neighborhood Dad is struck with guilt and remorse—cutting the devalue stage (or "training stage" as NashvilleKitty would describe it) short.

When I find a man worth molding, as I believed Neighborhood Dad to be a few seconds earlier, I consider him a "puppy." One day, such men could grow into loyal hounds, but they need to be trained. Time spent training them is worth the sacrifice when they show promise, but I have no interest in the runt of the litter. It looked like it wasn't me who was going to keep coming, but rather, his tears.

Discard: When NashvilleKitty no longer sees potential personal benefit from her relationship with Neighborhood Dad, she drops him like a hot potato. Neighborhood Dad is distraught over what he has done:

"This is my first time—I always imagined it, but I never thought about what would happen after."

He started to do that thing where he sobbed so violently his mucous mixed with his tears, and the whole mess looked like Depression-era porridge caked into his beard.

"I have a daughter. How could I have done this? What do I say to my wife?!"

I said nothing. You reach a point with neurotypical people where there's just no progress to be made. You cut your losses.

"Say something!" He shook as he screamed at me, like a toddler throwing a tantrum.

I threw his jeans at his face, muzzling him for a moment. Next came the belt and his shirt. I stood up and pulled my blouse back over my head, wishing I could pull hard enough to make him disappear by the time my eyes popped out the top. However, there he remained, a weeping mess on my floor.

"Can you hurry up?"

"Why? Is your husband coming home soon? Is he going to catch us?"

I ran over to him, bent at the waist, and whapped my opened palm against the back of his head. I wasn't going near the puddle on his face.

"No one is catching anyone. No one is saying a word to anybody. This never happened. I'll ruin your marriage and testify at your divorce if I start hearing any neighborhood rumors. Got it?"

He nodded and continued to snivel while staring at the floor.

Within the first chapter of the novel, NashvilleKitty is able to seduce, become bored by, and dump a new lover.

SEXOPATH LOVE CYCLE

| IDEALIZE | DEVALUE | DISCARD |

Empathy Lacking

Despite having a good time and enjoying the company of MrAverageJoe37069, NashvilleKitty has absolutely no empathy for him when he gets caught cheating by his wife.

If MrAverageJoe37069 had become a regular puppy of mine, I would never have allowed him to be so stupid about everything. Perhaps it was best he got caught when he did because my wrath would have been worse than the write-me-an-essay punishment he received from his wife. The experience was helpful, if only so I could be reminded of how important it was to find expert cheaters like me. I never replied to his message. As was always the case with people who appear to be 'nice,' they are among the most expectant for others to return the favor. I imagined him waiting for me to send a long reply—for both his and his wife's sakes—detailing all the ways he was a gentleman and why he should receive the most lenient sentence available. It's a classic neurotypical cycle. Kind people are some of the most selfish I've ever known. That's why I had to let him burn. I wouldn't be getting this puppy out of the pound. He got sacrificed—nice guys really do finish last.

Having a lack of empathy, means NashvilleKitty is unable to form connections with other people as the rest of us do. She discards anyone who does not satisfy her selfish aims.

She is incapable of feeling what another person feels—including love. NashvilleKitty believes that "No one knows what love is anyway," simply because she is not able to comprehend what love is. If she does not understand it, no one must, in her opinion. Love and empathy are impossible to understand if you have never experienced these feelings. Instead, NashvilleKitty aims to change the definition of love.

> *I don't need the internet to tell me that I love the way Hubby loves me—make a word for love of adoration and I'm in.*

Sexopaths cannot experience empathetic love—not now, not ever.

Breaks the law/
Changes the Rules

NashvilleKitty is always breaking her own rules as she does not believe rules apply to her. She also breaks the law by stealing money through her billing company. Here is a look into NashvilleKitty's criminal career where she clues us into how she does her work-from-home job and her reasoning behind it.

> *After LandscapeLover bounced away, I scurried off to my study with a fresh cup of spiked hot cocoa. After popping an Adderall to perk me up, I pulled out the spreadsheet to begin my monthly magic money-making ritual, and I'm not just talking about getting the employees paid properly. What so many people don't realize when it comes to medical insurance co-pays is doctors work too hard to pay attention to the financial details. That makes it incredibly easy to skim the cream off the top, especially with Medicare payments, where often the patients have a secondary insurance for the co-pays. Doctors were so excited to get the 80 percent from the government that they never noticed the missing co-pay. I enjoyed correcting this oversight on everyone's part,*

sipping spiked cocoa in my fuzzy socks, by funneling the co-pays of patients—which was no small sum when added all together— into my secret account. The beauty of working in healthcare— unlike the unfortunate souls who call themselves professional lawyers or auto mechanics—was the job came with a reputation for being a good, altruistic person. This status, like so many social constructions, had no basis in fact. Healthcare was full of people like me—although I do it better than most—who skim a little something for us from the huge pot of gold that people contribute to with the delusional hopes of health, or at least a pain-free death. The premium neurotypicals put on life was so high and the system so inefficient, it begged for smart people like me to come along and turn the job into something that gave us a lot more than a mere good reputation in the eyes of the citizenry—it gave us nice fat pockets. But hey, I deserve it.

As is typical of sexopaths, NashvilleKitty believes she is entitled to the money she steals—she thinks that if the neurotypicals are too stupid to notice, then that is their fault.

Sexopaths believe they deserve something just because they want it. In other words, they have limited control over their own impulses. To them, wanting something is reason enough to believe it's owed to them. When someone is behaving like this—having no impulse control when they are going after something they want—take notice that they are behaving like a sexopath.

Egotistical

NashvilleKitty thinks extremely highly of herself. She feels entitled to anything she wants exactly when she wants it. She is glib and feels superior to all of the people she manipulates on a daily basis.

The thing about religion is that it's strictly for neurotypicals. It really is the opium for the masses. Their weak minds and psychological limits necessitate their need to believe in a higher power to give some meaning to the events shaping their lives. Although I would never say it to their faces—it wouldn't play very well in my manipulation games, especially around these parts of the country—from everything I've gathered about the neurotypical concept of "God," I would consider myself on the same level.

Now, before you start fearing these words will catch on fire from God's wrath, let me explain. When things don't go the way neurotypicals want, they scramble for reasons why. After exhausting the blame they've put on themselves, others, and the

Come worship me for a while!

historical moment, they almost always turn to God. God, they say, has a plan. Well, you know what? I do too. If something is blocking me from following that plan, I simply remove it or change the rules so it no longer impedes me. When God removes a barrier in the life of a neurotypical, they praise God. When the same happens to me, I praise myself. Do you see, dear reader? I might not be <u>the</u> God these people keep referring to, but I clearly am <u>a</u> god—as is any other sexopath who knows how to use their abilities to the fullest.

NashvilleKitty is so egotistical that she actually believes she is a god.

Hollow Emotions

Sexopaths do not experience emotions like the rest of us. Having never experienced deep emotions, they have trouble understanding what they are.

It wasn't exactly intimacy in a traditional sense I craved. In fact, many say sexopaths are incapable of intimacy, per society's definition, and Lord knows all the emotion and togetherness wears on me. However, I do not think this means I cannot experience intimacy. I am married after all. Perhaps society's definition requires revision. I simply wish to be adored and not smothered. Is that too much to ask? I desire relationships with men who worship me, while respecting my space and providing intrigue by being a worthy match in intellect. Sex with the less-than-brilliant—as evidenced by my encounter with Neighborhood Cry Baby—has become simply random body parts colliding to make a sticky mess. With an intellectual equal—or at least an above-average man with a beautiful six-pack and those exquisite diagonal lines leading downward—I could have sex 24/7. That sounds intimate to me. In fact, I have always said that if I win the lottery, I will do nothing but have sex until I die. Show me one man who can keep up with that, and I will sell you the John Seigenthaler Bridge to walk on. Dating multiple men at once was the only satisfying option.

In this example, NashvilleKitty tries to change the definition of "intimacy" to mean "marriage" or "non-stop sex." She is incapable of understanding what empathetic intimacy is as she has never experienced it. The same is true for love.

Really, I don't do love in the traditional sense—it's a sexopathic prerogative. Even with Hubby, we didn't use the "L" word very often—only once or twice a year, tops, and usually because family members expected it. Puppies always fall in love with me as I mirror exactly what they wish to see. When it comes to love, I'm not infected. I'm just a carrier.

Love, what little I understood about it, was the tallest tale neurotypicals told themselves. Complete nonsense. From what I gathered, the word was supposed to represent all the comfortable things in life rolled into one—warmth, happiness, and ease. The fuzziness, as I heard it described, was supposedly desirable in that it made life's difficult moments less painful. Doesn't sound far-fetched enough yet, dear reader? Don't worry, there's more. The snake oil was somehow supposed to cure people of their inadequacies and gloss over the potholes on their life's journey to make everything a smooth ride.

Most neurotypicals used the word as a measure for the progress in their relationship. I used it as an indicator that a puppy had truly and fully been infected by a debilitating disease for which there exists no cure. The only upside to the word, as far as I was concerned, was that it basically served as a white flag for any sexopath paying attention. It was the ultimate surrender to manipulation.

NashvilleKitty has never experienced empathetic love and therefore tells herself that neurotypicals are simply lying to themselves. In one breath she admits she does not understand love, but in the next breath, she accuses the rest of us of making it all up. Since she sees deep emotions as weaknesses rather than something she is lacking, she plans to use everyone else's vulnerabilities for her own manipulative ends.

Irresponsible

Sexopaths are known for being irresponsible, unreliable, and often engage in a parasitic lifestyle by using others' willingness to take care of them to its full advantage. NashvilleKitty is no exception.

I have an awesome life with my doting husband. He pays my bills, does my laundry, buys my groceries, cooks most of my meals, and appropriately worships me in every way.

With their self-serving focus, sexopaths do not make the best parents. Children are often neglected or treated as possessions.

This is going to sound terrible—society has taught me not to say this aloud—but I don't like kids. They seem cute enough to look at when they are sleeping or even laughing, but poopy diapers and temper tantrums are as high on my no-no list as a full-time job.

The only person who can reliably depend on NashvilleKitty is NashvilleKitty. Serving herself is her main motivation in everything she does.

Not Me

Sexopaths never admit that anything is their fault—unless a insincere apology is the best manipulation technique for the present situation. However, fake apologies can be useful, particularly after being caught in a lie or a crime. Of course, even more enjoyable to sociopaths is attempting to turn the tables to place blame on anyone finding fault with the sexopath. NashvilleKitty redirects blame with new lies when Hubby comes home early from work. Just moments earlier, she had smoked marijuana and had sex with LandscapeLover in the basement shower.

"I sent a text right after lunch," Hubby said, answering my unasked question about why in God's name he was home before his usual scheduled time with no apparent warning. "Didn't you get it? Whose monster truck is that in the driveway?"

Crap. Must have been too high to look at my phone. "Yeah, I know! What is it about these landscape guys and their gaudy trucks?"

"We have new landscapers?"

"Yes, I told you about our neighbor who landscapes. Don't you listen to a word I say?"

"Of course, I do… Oh, wow. What's that smell? The last time I smelled that was when Miranda got you high. Is it coming from the basement?" He headed for the basement door, but I quickly cut him off as I turned the fault back on its head.

"That smell is you leaving the gate open and a skunk getting into the garbage! Instead of creating the Garden of Eden in the back yard, the landscape guy spent hours trying to get the stinky creature out. It stunk so bad, I had to shower to get the stench off me," I said, turning my nose upward in disgust.

"Whoops, sorry."

Turn the
table cuz
I'm able

When events on the cheaters' dating site begin to take a nasty turn, NashvilleKitty never once considers that her actions have contributed to her current situation. She never accepts blame.

SugarDaddy claimed to have so much money he traveled out of the country for a full six months out of the year. He traveled to wherever he wanted whenever he wanted. His recent trips included the Galapagos Islands, Thailand, and Barcelona. Getting away sounded good right about then. In fact, as we chatted, I decided that maybe I had been going about my puppy search the wrong way. By looking for sexual abilities first, I was going for the low hanging fruit. It became quite clear if my orchard was only limited to Nashville, the branches were too close to ground. Much of the fruit was rotten or bland, or both. If I found the right sugar daddy, maybe I could leverage his wealth to find more ripe and exotic fruit. That's it! It's not the kitty that's the problem—it's Nashville!

Sexopaths always blame others, circumstances—or in this case, an entire city.

Danger Seekers

Having no empathy means sexopaths do not spend time thinking about the needs of others. They have no regrets about the past and thoughts about the future go only as far as how to manipulate people to get their way. They find themselves in the present with a severe sensitivity to boredom and a need for excitement and danger.

Danger is something that thrills sociopaths and psychopaths alike—we get little joy out of life's mundane moments that seem to keep neurotypicals so content.

Having decreased fear, results in risk taking that most would consider unnecessary and unwise. After NashvilleKitty first failed date on Aubrey Madeline, she chooses to seek additional lovers on the cheaters' website with her husband in the next room.

I was bored—a sexopath's worst nightmare. I enjoy high-risk entertainment. It gives me a buzz. That's why, even with Hubby still up, I went to the study. I heard the TV from the living room as I logged into Aubrey Madeline.

ItalianStallion had left me a message, but having no fear of future consequences, I didn't even bother looking at it before I sent it to the trash. After all, what could he really do to me? Sue me for assault? He was just another reject added to the blocked list.

It is often in this reckless behavior to overcome boredom that the sexopath slips up and you are able to glimpse behind the mask.

What you don't seem to realize is how much control I have. Like all rules, mine are meant to be broken. If there is one thing I hate more than anything, it is having to wait for what I want. I am as calculated as they come. I am never going to get caught, but I am also not going to delay my satisfaction because of a little heightened risk. In fact, it turns me on.

NashvilleKitty overestimates her control. Her desire for danger mixed with her grandiose sense of self results in her taking risks that ultimately cause her downfall.

Targeting Next Victim

Sexopaths are always on the prowl in search of their next victim. NashvilleKitty modified her cheating strategy in order to assure instant gratification.

My original intention was to have one long-term, extra-marital affair with someone who lived out of town and came to Nashville for business. This seemed the safest scenario—don't sleep where you poop and all. The problem with this plan was my potential lover would not necessarily be available when I had free time and was looking for some satisfaction. Part of my definition of pleasure is getting what I want when I want it. The only time I believe in delayed gratification is to heighten my orgasm during sex. I quickly found that given the plethora of desperate married men, it worked best to have multiple studs and interchange them per availability. If the horses were not ready in their stables, all I had to do was log into the site for one day to visit the pony auction.

The supply seemed endless but presented a problem. Keeping track of all the men became more difficult as the number of conversations increased. I finally created a spreadsheet listing all the usernames and pertinent information about each one, including what I divulged about myself, such as my profession, special sexual details, who my family was, etc. I pride myself on a photographic memory, but it is easier to compare using Excel for assistance.

With a spreadsheet to keep track, NashvilleKitty always has the next potential lover ready and waiting.

Head Honcho

Often sexopaths in positions of power will use their power to coerce others to satisfy them sexually. NashvilleKitty enjoys control and power and considers her ability to select men from a large group of applicants on Aubrey Madeline as her own position of Human Resources hiring.

I become bored easily and finding a man who can hold my attention on multiple occasions can be difficult. Fortunately, there were so many men from which to choose. I adored having the luxury of being selective. From their standpoint, I must have seemed psychic, for I know when they were going to get lucky or not. And yes, I relish the power of deciding whether to allow access.

A sexopath in power will manipulate others for control. NashvilleKitty's parasitic lifestyle has not afforded her direct access to subordinates, but she does delight in controlling access to men.

Expressional Inconsistencies

Micro-inflections showing expressional inconsistencies can be a clue of an acting sexopath. NashvilleKitty feels anger that her first date on Aubrey Madeline has lied about his appearance and nationality. ItalianStallion is unattractive and French. If we had been looking at NashvilleKitty at this exact moment, we would have spotted her angry micro-inflections on her face before she regains control to reapply the mask.

> *Yet, before the date even began, I felt like punching him out, right there in the restaurant, to turn his face into a not-so-delicate American interpretation of Italian cuisine. As the waiter arrived to take our drink order, I restrained myself. Remember: sexopath emotions are a light switch.*

It is in the seconds before sexopaths flip the switch back to "calm and collected" that you may see the flash of anger in their eyes. By being observant, you may glimpse behind the mask.

Sexopaths can be caught trying to act empathetically as we see in the following NashvilleKitty example that occurs minutes after NashvilleKitty slept with LandscapeLover for the last time and then dumped him. Having fallen head over heels in love with NashvilleKitty who refused to respond to his messages, LandscapeLover made a scene by honking his horn outside her house until NashvilleKitty let him in. As she sees sleeping with him as the best way to get rid of him, NashvilleKitty plays a game to see how quickly she can have sex with him, and then she dumps him. She watches his love turn to hate as she discards this no-longer-useful-lover.

> *The doorbell rang only a few minutes later. I figured he forgot something so I didn't even bother to check the peep hole. I didn't want him getting any more neighborhood attention. I opened the door to find his wife's pockmarked face inches from mine.*
>
> *"Where is he?" she demanded.*
>
> *"Your husband?" I asked, smugly.*
>
> *Yes!"*

"I believe that is your job to know, not mine," I said. "He is just my former landscaper but, as you know, all the landscaping I needed is done."

She folded her arms. "I know he has feelings for you," she said, holding back sobs. "He told me himself."

"Rest assured, I am a happily married woman. You have nothing to worry about from me." I forced a smile and reached to cup her elbow. I heard grabbing someone's elbow when they're upset was the best way to make them feel at ease. She yanked her arm away immediately.

Maybe I heard wrong.

"He's never been this way before he met you. You've destroyed him. You're a monster playing with his emotions. You think this is a game, but it's not. He has a lot at stake." She was crying. "He has a family. He has children. They need someone to look up to—not someone who is going to run off with a slut!"

I had nothing to say to her, but I needed her off my doorstep as fast as I could. Between the honking husband and the weeping wife, any nosy neighbors had more than enough ammunition for the night.

"I'm sure he is just out on a job. Go home," I said, taking a big sigh before uttering one of the biggest lies of my life. "You have nothing to worry about. He is a good man."

"He is my man," she said, storming off my doorstep. "Get your own!"

"Believe me, lady," I whispered to myself after she left. "I will!"

NashvilleKitty calculates how to appear empathetic by touching the woman's elbow and saying what the wife wants to hear in order to get her off her doorstep.

Magnetism

Sexopaths are known for their superficial charm and magnetism. They often seem bigger than life and attract people to them as a moth to a flame. NashvilleKitty is no exception. One of her most effective weapons is mirroring. The following is how she fooled LandscapeLover into becoming her obedient puppy.

His adoration for me quickly grew, and I could not fault him on his excellent taste. So often my puppies were so starved for the slightest attention that it took very little to earn their undying love and devotion. I have also mastered the delicate art of mirroring— as every good sexopath should—where I allow the other person to talk ad nauseam while I mirror back what they say. I reveal nothing of what I believe but merely parrot back so the speaker reaches the incorrect conclusion that I agree with everything discussed. People do not adore you for who you are but for how you make them feel. Sexopaths are known for being adept at imitating the mannerisms of other people to hide their own personalities. Even if I change my outer personality as frequently as I change my clothes, I can still appreciate my great inner self-worth. I know I am amazing, as my puppies keep reminding me.

By projecting back whatever a person wishes to see, sexopaths are able to foster loyal followers yearning for more false flattery.

Anger

Sexopaths tend to have fits of illogical rage over trivial things. In the following example, NashvilleKitty becomes enraged by ChainReaction—although she hides her reaction from him until she is able to exact her revenge.

I narrowed my eyes on him.

"It will be all right," he added in a very parental tone. "Don't be scared."

"You know, the last time someone talked to me in a voice like that, I threatened to expose him to his wife," I said, feeling my body heating up.

"What?" he asked, suddenly looking quite scared himself.

"My dad tried to tell me to keep the baby when I got pregnant in high school, and I threatened to tell my mom about his cheating," I said without a shred of emotion. "So, don't try to patronize me."

ChainReaction spread his hands out wide.

"Don't you see?" he said. "You're doing the exact same thing as him."

"Excuse me?" I said, starting to keep mental score of all the things he said for which he needed to be reprimanded.

"You are doing the same thing to your sister as your dad did to you."

"Except his advice was bad and mine is good."

"Whatever," he said. "I forgot you guys are both sexopaths who are here to control us helpless neurotypicals. Obviously, you are going to think you're right."

That's the last straw. He wasn't finished either.

"Look, I know you're usually the one giving me advice—and I know I need a lot of it—but sexopath or not, I think you have some major issues to work out with your dad. It's influencing everything in your life, especially how you're treating your sister during the time she needs you most."

I hoped it wouldn't come to this. He has crossed the line and must be punished.

NashvilleKitty's reaction is over the top and what follows afterwards is even more disturbing and vindictive.

Sex Addiction

Sexopaths are known to be prone to addictions of all sorts. NashvilleKitty is addicted to sex as well as alcohol and amphetamines.

In high school, I provided anyone eager to give me oral pleasure the opportunity. What did I have to lose? This philosophy led to all sorts of quickie adventures in dirty school bathrooms, broom closets, and trash-filled cars. Beneath the bleachers, with their wonderful acoustics, was another favorite location. You name a place, and someone probably went down on me there. I stopped wearing underwear by fifteen to facilitate oral encounters. It was also arousing when my tight jeans rubbed against my naked flesh. My nickname was "Little Caesar"—not because of my strategic mind or being cheap and cheesy—but because I was always hot and ready.

NashvilleKitty uses her sex addiction as a justification for her infidelity.

I have a very high sex drive and need repeated satisfaction. As far as I can tell, sex—when done correctly—is one of the best things about being alive. Hubby loves me and wants to please me, but my sexual needs would send him to the hospital if he attempted to fully satisfy me. Having multiple affairs has always been the only option.

Sex addiction for sexopaths is often about control and conquest.

How do I keep a man going until I'm satisfied? It's all a matter of control.

One reason addiction may be so common in sexopaths is because it is a way to fight the boredom of having no empathy.

Kill for Power and Control

Sexoopaths will kill (figuratively—and sometimes literally) to maintain power and control. They want to win the game at all costs.

Didn't I mention that I have no patience to play if I'm not the game master?

Having power and control even outweighs NashvilleKitty's recurrent desire for sexual gratification.

I wasn't busy at all. In fact, I'm never too busy for an orgasm. What LandscapeLover had to learn—and what he had witnessed through the window—was that all puppies must obey their master.

Her need to manipulate is stronger than her sexual addiction.

I always said the only thing better than an orgasm was a masterful manipulation—and ChainReaction was my favorite marionette.

In the end, power and control trump everything else in NashvilleKitty's life.

The bottom line was I needed to regain control. TenSin had taken power away from me. Without it, I was nothing—almost as bad as any run-of-the-mill, sad neurotypical on the street. Popular culture insisted compassion was the way to salvation, that being kind to others would set you free, that we were all created equal and should treat each other as such. Well, if I haven't convinced you we all are not created equally, then you might be worse off than I thought. Power is a zero-sum game—you either lose it or you gain it. It was a pup-eat-pup world out there, and this kitty was not one to fight for scraps.

Despite her repeated claims that she is nonviolent, NashvilleKitty acted violently with ChainReaction and openly speaks of her plans for vengeance.

That's where my path differs from Scarlett's. When I do get out—and trust me, I will get out—I won't be going backward. I won't be going back to Tara—forget Rhett. I will do whatever it takes to find the person responsible for putting me in here. They stripped me of power, but even more importantly, they've taken away the one resource no one can get back. Time is something even sexopaths can't manipulate. They've robbed time from me—so much pleasure sacrificed, so many puppies left wandering the streets alone without a kitty to train them. If Scarlett O'Hara taught me anything, it's that we must be willing to do whatever it takes to preserve our way of life. My right to be a sex loving sexopath is under attack. Whoever is responsible will feel my vengeance and get what they deserve.

NashvilleKitty has all the characteristics of a sexopath and is an excellent example of a sociopathic sex addict.

POWER IS A ZERO-SUM GAME

MORE FOR ME = LESS FOR YOU

NashvilleKitty is a Sexopath - One Among Many

The purpose of the Sexopath Spotting Tool is to give you an honest assessment of a person's behavior. As red flags stack up, so does the likelihood the person in question is a sexopath (or at least behaves sexopathically often enough for it to be a problem). How many traits are enough to deem the person a full-blown sexopath? That's up to your discretion. There are no hard and fast rules. After all, these are people we're dealing with. What The Spotting Tool provides is a guide by which to grade questionable behavior. It is then up to you to decide how to interact with someone. Would I allow NashvilleKitty access to my heart, my family, or my wallet? No, I would not. She is a sexopath—and now you and I have the tool to spot her!

Chapter 7: Taking the Power Back and Keeping It

Sandra is struggling to understand her friend Candice. They've known each other for years, since they were freshmen in high school. They graduated from the same business and computer engineering double degree program and even were both hired together for entry level positions at their dream tech start up.

The first few months everything seemed normal, then Candice started to treat Sandra differently. Where before she asked Sandra's opinion and advice on work and life dilemmas during their private one-on-one lunchbreak sessions, now Candice seemed to prefer to eat lunch in groups with their new coworkers.

Candice seemed to be able to sway the conversation according to whatever whim she had for the day. Mostly, these were topics that suited her or a project she was working on—or, even more commonly, a guy she was interested in at the company.

Another thing that began to irk Sandra was the way her friend would avoid meetings where problems were going to be discussed about a project or new piece of software. She'd call in sick, take an extended lunch, or have another project manager sign off on her to work with a different team. What was weird, at least from Sandra's perspective, was that a lot of the problems that arose during those meetings were because of mistakes Candice made in her lines of code. During college, she rarely made these sort of mistakes—Sandra remembers because they did all the work together, with Sandra's double checking everything for both of them. In the context of school work, it was something Sandra was happy to do for her friend, but in the working world she was juggling too much to double check all of Candice's work before they submitted it to the project manager. Sandra often covered for Candice, even when she wasn't at the meetings, shouldering some of the blame herself, but there were times when the mistakes were so blatant that Sandra didn't want to compromise her own standing at the company by admitting to the errors.

SOCIOPATHS USE A "LOYAL FRIEND" TO COVER THEIR SLOPPY WORK ETHIC

One day after a particularly brutal meeting on a project, Sandra asked Candice about the mistakes she'd made in her code. Candice became very defensive and somehow turned the tables to blame Sandra for the entire situation. Sandra tried to backpedal away before the argument got heated, but it was too late. Candice gave her a hard stare and stormed from the room.

Similar issues kept happening on company projects, until one day, Sandra came across a more disturbing scene. After coming back from a doctor's appointment, she parked two spaces down from Candice, hoping the proximity to their parking would force the two to have a friendly interaction, like the friends they used to be. Sandra didn't even think about how strange it was that Candice's car was parked so far away in the corner of the parking garage. When Sandra got out of the car, however, she immediately understood why. Candice's legs were over her head, as she was getting drilled by one of the project supervisors. Impossible to turn away, Sandra stood there watching until she and Candice locked eyes. It was the first time they'd looked directly at each other since before their big fight. Instead of anger, Candice simply paused her pleasure writhing face, winked at Sandra and dragged her tongue along the project manager's neck.

That image was burned into Sandra's head the rest of that day and the following week. Candice didn't say a word to her about it but quickly began to make intimate moves toward the other higher-ups in the company. One day Candice walked toward the Chief Financial Officer's office, which sat adjacent to Sandra's desk. As Sandra watched, Candice rubbed her hand against the CFO's crotch at his stand-up desk with a sideways smirk, then she glanced over at Sandra as she did it, who looked away immediately. Sandra's heart began to beat so fast, she thought it would crack her ribcage.

What the hell am I supposed to do? Why is she doing this? How does she expect me to react?

Candice's behavior continued to occupy Sandra's mind at the office and at night for sleepless hours. She didn't know who this person was. Through their entire friendship, Candice had hardly talked about sex. It was true that their time together was usually at class or studying, but Sandra always assumed Candice lived a relatively quiet life like she did. It wasn't like they were best friends that knew everything about each other, but Sandra always felt they represented a solid, positive force in each other's work pursuits. They motivated each other. They were work buds.

The more she thought about it all, the worse Sandra did at work. She began to make the mistakes she had only lied about before on Candice's behalf. Her sleep schedule became erratic, and she stopped eating meals regularly because she didn't want to see Candice at lunch. When several of her work projects began to have serious problems, she was asked by the Chief Executive Officer's secretary to set up an appointment about her job performance.

In the days leading up to the meeting, Sandra worked herself into a state of absolute hysteria. She even had a panic attack one day before work and went to the Emergency Department. As she lay there, heavily medicated, trying to slowly retrace her steps and figure out what happened, the nurse announced she had a visitor. It was Candice.

Heavily sedated, Sandra couldn't even reach her hand up to tell Candice to go away. As Candice set down a vase of flowers, she smiled and laid on the same charm that she had when they first met in high school. She pretended nothing had happened and didn't acknowledge her recent sexual behavior. Candice continued to make small talk about office projects and then kissed Sandra on the forehead, whispering, "Remember, I am always loyal to you," before the nurse escorted her out.

"It must be so nice," the nurse said to Sandra once Candice had left, "to have such a kind friend and colleague in your life."

For the rest of the day, Sandra tried to convince herself that the nurse was right.

Candice was a good friend. She was a good colleague. Who cares about the sexual stuff? Everyone has their dark side. Sandra needed to get back to how things were with Candice. Without her, who was Sandra anyway?

In her sedated state, Sandra rationalized the situation. After all, she thought, Candice had always been the more attractive, more charismatic of the two. She probably had put in a good word for Sandra to even get the job in the first place. Sandra owed so much to Candice, how dare she question her friend or try to point to problems in her code at work.

Candice was not the problem, she decided. *I am the problem.*

When Sandra went back to work the next week, Sandra happily resumed doing double the work to check the code Candice had been assigned for projects. Candice continued her sexual exploits with coworkers, with Sandra helping cover for her when colleagues inquired into her long lunch breaks. Never for a second did Sandra ever consider she might be doing the wrong thing. She just accepted her fate as Candice's accomplice—even if it meant working herself into another panic attack.

WHEN EMPATHS ARE VULNERABLE SOCIOPATHS WILL MANIPULATE

EMPATHS BELIEVE THE BEST ABOUT PEOPLE – FORGETTING THE FACTS

How to Survive in a Sexopathic World

Common sense says to stay away from people who lack empathy and a conscience. Then why is it that we, like Sandra, so often gravitate towards sociopaths or even empower them in our lives? Much of this can be explained by hope. We hope that we can help them grow to become "better people." Although there is some promising research with interventions in young children while the brain has greater plasticity, the same is not possible with adults. Now, with the science of neurobiology, we realize that some people are incapable of becoming more empathetic, conscientious people. We need not risk the negative effects to ourselves, our families, and our lives by continuing to hold out hope that those acting sociopathically amongst us will somehow change.

Since sociopaths are not going to be cured or disappear, it's undoubtedly better to figure out how to deal with their continued existence. Let's accept reality as it is, and figure out what to do next. Instead of clinging to false hope that they will change, it's far more practical and productive to consider ways we can identify sociopaths who currently exist, and then learn how to interact with them.

Having recognized sociopaths in our lives, we need to open up the discussion as to what to do next. We want to find appropriate ways to interact with them even while we idealistically hope that someday we will be able to activate their empathy and conscience. Who knows what the future holds, but for now, this is our reality.

In my novel, *69 Shades of Nashville*, my protagonist NashvilleKitty describes what happened to her former lover ChainReaction towards the end of the book (and let's just say it wasn't something kind). She feels no remorse but rather almost brags of her manipulation, lack of empathy, and blatant disregard for the fate he ended up enduring. As wise readers, we recognize NashvilleKitty for what she is—while all her fellow characters fail to identify her. After all, they don't have the benefit of The Sexopath Spotting Tool to help them. They, like Sandra in our example above, have no tools and stood no chance when placed in the wrecking ball of a sexopath.

THERE IS NO CURE

Take two of these and still NOT feel me in the morning!

Interacting with Sociopaths and Sexopaths: A Dangerous Sport

Identifying sexopathy is one thing, learning how to interact with sociopaths and sexopaths is another. While keeping in mind that the purpose of The Sexopath Spotting Tool is only to help protect you from sociopathic and sexopathic behavior—which often results in sexual misconduct, rape, and violent attacks in personal and professional settings—it's important to also consider setting up an overall defensive structure to help avoid getting caught up in a sociopath or sexopath's game.

Know Yourself: Vulnerabilities Become Strengths

Sociopaths use their keen observational skills to pinpoint your weaknesses and vulnerabilities. Ironically, they often understand you better than you understand yourself. Frequently, self-examination and soul-searching are pretty low on our To Do Lists—empathetic people are too busy being concerned with the daily trials of family and friends—but the number one way you can protect yourself and those you love from manipulation is to know yourself. What pushes your buttons? What are your hopes and dreams? Your fears or insecurities? Self-examination helps you discover your vulnerabilities. Everybody has them and sharing them is part of a normal, healthy relationship with someone who has earned your trust. By knowing your vulnerabilities, you can more easily recognize when someone is exploiting them.

Often, it is difficult to get to know yourself in a vacuum. Since self-reflection alone generally does not always produce effective results, friends and family often can give you a different perspective—although be aware that sometimes they are too close to the situation to give clear advice. Sometimes we need to talk to someone who simply has more experience than our friends and family, someone trained to help people work through problems. A psychotherapist can help you become knowledgeable about your vulnerabilities while helping you sort through your close relationships. It doesn't make you weak or crazy to talk with a professional who can help you sort through the manipulations of a sociopath and expose the destructive and often repetitive patterns in your life. Many insurance plans cover psychotherapy, yet most people do not take advantage of this valuable service.

It is important to find the right therapist. After seeing the first counselor a few times, if it doesn't feel right then try another. Think of it like finding the right winter coat—keep trying on coats until you find the right fit. Depending on the type of therapist, you may be given suggestions to try outside of therapy. Part of human nature is to understand intellectually what is best for us, but then still resist change with all of our might. It is our Inner Rebel. Be aware of this tendency, and choose to live your life on purpose. You have power over your decisions and actions. Use your power.

Hearing kind words of appreciation can warm your soul. Most of us work hard to help others, yet no one seems to notice or care. Although we all deserve to be recognized for how we make the world a little bit better, often the empathetic majority is so caught up in the chaos of life to remember to appreciate our finer actions. Frequently, sociopaths use this fact to their advantage with false flattery about your abilities and talents. Even those who study sociopaths for a living can fall prey to their charm. Sociopaths will ask you questions to figure out what motivates you and use any vulnerabilities they might find for manipulation—often with your being completely unaware. Granted, it is very tedious to always be on guard when you are around someone who might be a sociopath, but it is absolutely necessary. Sociopaths use our emotions against us. They want you to trust them, so it is up to you to be rational rather than emotional when dealing with them. People need to earn your trust—not with pleasing words but with provable actions.

Examine how you define "respect." Do you confuse fear with respect? Sociopaths can be bullies who use fear and intimidation to force others into submission. They are predators frightening their prey. Respect should be reserved for those who are kind and morally brave—those who are willing to do what is right even when it is not personally beneficial. If you are always walking on eggshells to avoid a sociopath's anger, then you fear this person—that is not the same as respect.

What is your relationship with guilt? Although sociopaths feel no guilt, they enjoy using your guilt against you. Notice if someone in your life is always making you feel guilty—especially if your guilt is manipulated to make you do things not in your own self-interest. The same is true for pity. Is someone always using the pity card to excuse misbehavior? Sociopaths use all these emotions to make you feel crazy to a point where you question your own sanity. They are masters of psychological blackmail. Examine when and why you feel these emotions, and if they seem to always originate from the same individual, pay close attention for manipulation attempts. Know yourself. Acknowledging which buttons make you react makes you much less susceptible to sociopathic abuse.

Listen to Your Gut—Use Your Head

Trust your gut. The empathetic majority has an incredible talent to feel what others feel. Empathy is our strength, yet few of us appreciate its power. Our deep emotions and physical responses give us clues to danger—if only we are brave enough to listen. Ask yourself, "How does this person make me feel?" and observe any physical sensations in your body. Is there something about this person that just seems "off," but you are not sure what? When a sociopath is in full charm mode, our conscious mind is enjoying the false flattery ride while our deeper instincts detect the truth. When we are in danger, our primal brain kicks into action to warn us. Our subconscious picks up seemingly insignificant details that our conscious mind did not even register as significant while our body responds with physical signals to tell us to beware. Is your skin crawling? Heart racing? Stomach turning? Do you feel like prey? Listen to your body. If ever you have a sense of danger, get away. If possible, leave without attracting attention, but don't risk your safety because of a fear of being rude.

First impressions are hard to shake. We decide what we think about a person in the first moments we meet and will often ignore future evidence that contradicts that first impression. There is part of us that wants so badly for our first impressions to be right. Sociopaths know this and are experts at wearing the perfect mask for every situation. With them, what you see is not reality. If you are anxious, the sociopath is reassuring and soothing. If you are narcissistic, the sociopath feeds your desire for admiration. If you are lonely, the sociopath offers companionship and excitement. Beware of instant uninvited intimacy. Sociopaths are incapable of experiencing true intimacy which takes time to develop. Instead, they will try to create the illusion of immediate intimacy. Joe Navarro makes an excellent point about the difference between niceness and goodness. Niceness is about actions anyone can perform regardless of what is hidden in the heart. Goodness is about character and intentions. Assess for goodness by seeking out the intentions behind behaviors.

Often people will reveal you who they are if you are paying attention. Listen to their words and compare them to their actions. Are there inconsistencies? Watch out for facts and details that don't quite fit what was said or done on prior occasions. Sociopaths tend to be inconsistent in little moments when the mask begins to slip. Pay attention to the way someone acts when there is nothing observable to gain. For example, how does

TRUST YOUR GUT

OBSERVE YOUR
PHYSICAL REACTIONS

someone treat a waiter, cashier, or stranger on the street? What about being sweet to the in-laws in person but then complaining bitterly when they leave? Is the mask different in different settings? Be willing to shift your point of view as you collect more information about what a person is really like. Take it a step further and do some fact checking. With the help of the internet, you can verify or discredit the charmer's stories. Before you allow a stranger access to your heart, your children, or your pocketbook—make sure the stories match. Have a qualified professional examine any contracts or financial deals before you commit—spend a little now to save so much more both financially and emotionally if it turns out to be a sociopathic scam. I have said it before, but it begs repeating—people must earn your trust.

Face Facts - Stop With the Excuses

Once you identify multiple red flags (predatory stare, obvious lack of empathy, skirting responsibility, recurrent lies, blames others, etc.) especially over a period of time, trust the spotting tool and be honest in your assessment. You don't need to diagnosis anyone or hand out any labels, but if you have discovered that someone is a pathological liar capable of manipulation and deceit—that is more than enough to warrant additional boundaries when dealing with this person. The facts speak for themselves.

Resist the urge to make excuses for sociopathic actions or fall for their lies aimed to minimize their behavior. Be careful of the tendency to both listen to excuses about their behavior (which they will undoubtedly make, usually served with a side helping of charm) and making excuses for them on your own (because, like Sandra, you don't want to kick such a charismatic, exciting friend/lover to the curb). Question their pitiful (probably fictional) life story while remembering that others with a traumatic past do not all lie, cheat, and steal. Regardless of the past, people make choices and are responsible for their actions. Your pity does not give sociopaths a free pass, so do not make excuses for them. Your life, or at least your happiness, is at stake.

Denial can be very powerful—especially when the sociopath keeps whispering lies of loyalty—but you can save yourself so much pain if you accept sociopaths for who they are. Sociopaths have an almost hypnotic ability to make you believe. So often we simply do not want to accept that someone we trust is actually a sociopath. Empathetic people, myself included, want to see the best in people. The thought of falsely accusing someone is repulsive. What if we are wrong? Empathetic people question themselves constantly—our justice system is based on innocent until proven guilty. However, we have to face the facts. If the evidence points to multiple sociopathic characteristics, we need to be wary.

If you are in a rollercoaster relationship swinging from highs to lows at breathtaking speeds, it may be time to face facts that you may be dealing with a sociopath. Sociopaths may be completely devoted to you one day but then suggest you are disposable the next. When someone alternates between hot and cold extremes, your moods tend to follow that course, making you feel emotionally imbalanced. It may be severely disappointing to think this person in whom you have invested so much of your time, money, and emotional energy is simply using you, but the sooner you face this reality, the sooner your suffering will end.

Talk to Other Empathetic People: United We Stand

The empathetic majority greatly outnumber the sociopaths. We can take our power back by working together in our awareness of those without conscience. Sociopaths can't tell the same lie to everyone. Frequently, people will suspect someone of being a sociopath (or, at least, a pathological, manipulative liar) but no one is brave enough to discuss it. Often the sociopath has everyone swimming in self doubt, uncertainty, and fear—it is one of the sociopath's most effective tools—so the only way to deal with the situation is for people to have open discussion.

Sociopaths understand the danger of empathetic communication and will often try to keep people compartmentalized and divided. They delight in pitting groups against each other. Sociopaths' greatest fear is being discovered because they know they are not like the rest of us. If they can get empathetic people fighting among each other, there is less risk of detection and retaliation.

Suspect anyone who tries to isolate you. Sociopaths use both physical and emotional isolation to control their victims. For example, never get into a stranger's car, even if they have a weapon or give you an emotionally fraught reason that they need you. Once you are in the car and taken to a secondary site, your chances of survival are markedly decreased. Kick, yell, scream, bite, scratch, and resist in any way you can but, even if they have a gun—DON'T GET IN THE CAR!!! You are more likely to survive a gunshot wound outside the car, than have a favorable outcome if the stranger takes you to a remote location.

Develop your own support team. Communicate with other empathetic people about the sociopathic traits you see in an individual so that you can compare notes and expose the lies. If someone tells you that a friend made an insulting remark about you, go to the friend and ask for the truth. It may be a simple misunderstanding or you may find that the person spreading nasty gossip is actually a liar. Either way, it is better to get the information from the actual source rather than carry resentment against your friend without all the facts. By communicating, we can prevent the sociopath's plan to pit friend against friend.

Unfortunately, sociopaths are not usually held accountable for the physical, emotional, psychological, and financial suffering they cause. Most victims do not report sociopaths to authorities because of the shame they feel for being manipulated. Corporations do not prosecute as they fear it may damage their reputations. Sociopaths simply move on to new settings to target new empathetic souls to torture. With a new era of communication and openness, this vicious cycle can stop.

SOCIOPATH EXPOSED

Three Strikes and You're Out!

If you're unsure about whether someone is a sociopath based on an interaction or two (just as everybody makes mistakes, everybody has the potential to behave sociopathically or sexopathically with the right mixture of substance or circumstance), give the person another chance but, like an umpire, level the playing field with a three-strike rule. If they lie, manipulate, deceive, or show a lack of empathy three times, then that person needs to be cut loose. It may be difficult, but it is far better to do it as soon as possible. Remember, you are wasting your empathetic resources by holding on to the relationship; so stop making excuses for sociopaths and move on.

Avoidance For Safety

If possible, just steer clear of sociopaths when you recognize their behavior. The safest interaction is no interaction. Keep off their radar and avoid all contact if you can. Granted, this may be more challenging for people who work with sociopaths, have them in their families, or must engage with them in certain social settings, but is still the best approach when feasible.

Establishing no contact with a sociopath can be tricky. One of the worst things you can do is confront them about their lack of empathy as this may result in anger and possible violence or retaliation toward you. It is best to avoid them in a quiet and unobtrusive manner. M.E. Thomas suggests that the proper way to break up with a sociopath is to make it seem like it was the sociopath's idea. Become overly needy and emotional. Stop bathing. Become intolerable to live with. Act depressed and become incompetent. It may take a few months, but eventually the sociopath will leave you. This may be easier said than done, but it is an interesting approach to obtaining your freedom.

Mess with the prickly, and you will get poked!

FORM BOUNDARIES

YOU DESERVE RESPECT NOT VICTIMIZATION

Boundaries for Peace of Mind

Sometimes, complete avoidance is not possible and you must establish boundaries to protect yourself, your relationship, and your family. This means it is ok to say no. In our society, the urge to be nice and polite can lead to our downfall. Having boundaries does not mean you are unloving, mean, or selfish. In fact, boundaries are a form of self-respect and can protect what is important to you. When you have weak boundaries, you will put up with just about anything to feel loved. Stop that. You deserve better.

Never lie for a sociopath. The crocodile tears may be flowing as sociopaths beg you not to reveal their manipulations. They will lay on the guilt and prey on your pity. "It will never happen again" or "Please don't tell" may be the urgent pleas of sociopaths trying to convince you to ignore your conscience as they claim "You owe me" or "You are just like me." Don't believe them. You are different because you have empathy. Do not allow your good nature to be manipulated to hide the true character of a sociopath. By doing so, you are continuing the cycle of abuse and others will be hurt by your misplaced pity.

If you must work with sociopaths (a more and more common occurrence in corporate America), maintain your guard. Sociopaths are devious by nature and are always trying to manipulate the system. Keeping detailed records of what is said and done is essential if you need to prove the truth against a charming cheater. Demand transparency and accountability. Even thought it's unpleasant to be a "tattle-tale," make sure you voice your concerns to higher management early on if possible—before the sociopath is able to discredit you and turn the tables. Communication is key and documented evidence of how a sociopath is costing the corporation money may be the best approach. Sociopaths have no concept of social boundaries and attempt to bully and negate you without giving it a second thought. However, they will act like a constitutional lawyer if they think their rights have been violated. To sociopaths, rules only count when they serve their agenda. Keep track of the inconsistencies.

Don't allow yourself to be pressured or rushed. Sociopaths often use a sense of urgency to decrease your defenses and get you to act without examining all the facts. Slow things down. Take your time. Allow yourself to think and consult with others. When people pressure you to make a decision before you are ready, there is a high likelihood they are not thinking of your best interests. When people truly care, they will respect your desire to slow things down in order to make an informed choice. Set boundaries to make decisions on your own timeline.

Predators can pick easy victims by how they walk. When you are in public, be alert and make eye contact with people to let them know you see them. Try not to be on your phone and distracted, but walk with confidence with a hand free in case for extra protection. Consider taking a self-defense class. Pay attention to your surroundings. When we lived in small villages and everyone knew each other, sociopaths were easily recognized. Living in cities where neighbors are unknown, sociopaths hide in plain sight. Being aware and on guard has never been more important.

What if your child is a future sociopath? When dealing with a child with sociopathic traits, firmness and consistency is absolutely necessary—not only for the child but for the entire family. Often it is easier to simply give in to the child's demands in order to avoid further arguments, but this temporary relief comes at a cost. Sociopathic children zone in on adults lacking boundaries. They see permissiveness as signs that an adult is weak and can be manipulated. These children are always testing their limits. Their pattern of behavior is to do whatever is easiest to obtain their goal, looking for loopholes as they take a mile for every inch of freedom given. Children need to know what is expected of them and what the consequences will be for irresponsible behavior. The key is to figure out what is important to the child and use that as a means of fostering acceptable behavior. For example, make clear that lying is not acceptable and that a lie will result in no internet access until the child is able to demonstrate responsible behavior. Everyone knows what is expected and what the consequences will be. Of course, this works much better with empathetic children who learn from mistakes and fear punishment. Budding sociopathic children actually may be more motivated to conform to societal expectations by using bribes rather than threats of punishment since they seek the reward more than they fear penalty. If you think you may have a child with sociopathic tendencies, it is imperative to seek help from professionals with specific expertise in this field. These children will never grow up to be angels, but with early intervention, they are more likely to become functional and productive members of society.

FUTURE SOCIOPATH

In all cases, if someone refuses to respect your boundaries and attempts to force you to do something with which you are uncomfortable, just say no. Trust your gut and stick by your decision. They may leave angry, but instead of feeling guilty or worrying that you hurt their feelings—not even possible because sociopaths have no feelings to hurt—feel proud that you maintained your boundaries and protected yourself. Respecting yourself leads to increased respect from others. Sociopaths will do as much as you will allow them to get away with. Have firm boundaries and stick to them to keep yourself and those you love safe.

Don't Try to Change a Sociopath - It's Pointless

The urge to change a sociopath into someone with empathy may seem like an honorable goal, but you are simply wasting your time. Nothing you do or say will change them; you cannot correct the faulty connections within their brains, and the energy you spend trying to change a sociopath is a wasted investment. You cannot get on with your own life until you accept this fundamental fact: THEY WILL NEVER CHANGE. Additionally, there are people more deserving of your love and hope, and your energies are better spent where they can actually help someone to grow into a better person.

Despite what sociopaths may think, you cannot control another person's behavior. People are responsible for their own choices and decisions. You can change yourself, but you cannot force someone else to change. It is outside your control and trying to do so is pointless. If you want to help people, then help those who are open to being helped. Sociopaths seek to manipulate your kind intentions to benefit themselves. You cannot fix them—so don't waste your time and emotional energy trying.

It is a mistaken belief that love conquers all. Most of us are capable of deep, empathetic love and believe that with that love, we can change any situation. This simply is not the case with sociopaths. Those without conscience have no empathetic love to give so it becomes a one way street when you give your love to a sociopath. Their goal is not an equal relationship. Since they wish to dominate and control, giving your love to a sociopath will only harm you in the end. The stronger your boundaries are, the more you have to give to those whom you love and who truly care about you. In reality, self-care is essential to helping others. Eliminating toxic people from your life does not make you selfish—it enables you to be more giving to those who can actually reciprocate your love.

Remember - Empathy Leads to Forgetting

Time inevitably passes between your interactions with sociopaths, and it is the tendency of the human brain to forget the evidence you have collected in your interactions with them. It is important to remember everything (your own experiences, The Sexopath Spotting Tool, lies told, manipulations revealed) when it comes to sociopathy. Do not get caught in a place where you forget the always present danger—now more than ever. REMEMBER—THEY WILL NEVER CHANGE.

Write things down. Having a personal journal or sending yourself an email detailing the evidence of sociopathy will help you remember why your boundaries are so important—and it may save you in a courtroom. Many divorce cases are won by having records of the sociopath's abuse. Written records trump faulty memories or sociopathic lies every time.

Sociopaths are known for their ability to shower you with affection when they need something, and it is easy to forget all of the abuse when the charm is flowing. Consider keeping a list of the reasons why you need to have your guard up with this person and pull the list out to remind yourself whenever necessary. Call a trusted friend to remind you of your lessons learned. When sociopaths play the pity card, remember that regardless of the past, people are responsible for the decisions they make today. Do not accept excuses for irresponsibility. You may be seeing the attractive exterior of the perfect person now, but never forget the glimpses behind the mask.

In summary, when you are tempted to let your guard down, remind yourself of the inconsistencies. Look at their actions rather than the words. Examine the little moments when the mask slips and true character is revealed. Remind yourself that there truly are people without conscience and the inability to feel empathy. Remember that appearances are deceiving. A sociopath creates your perfect illusion while internally thinking you are weak for having emotions. Your empathetic love will never be returned by a sociopath. Don't waste your energy on someone incapable of giving back.

Time makes you forget

REMEMBER THE SOCIOPATH'S TRUE NATURE

Don't Try to Outsmart a Sociopath - You Might Lose

Avoid the pitfall of dropping to the sociopath's level. You can't outsmart a sociopath all the time. While you might be successful occasionally, the consequence of being outsmarted even once simply does not justify the risks of interacting with them. There's the temptation that if they seem to be of average intelligence, you think you can outsmart them or beat them at their own game. Just remember that they do not waste energy on emotions or caring and their determination to win may give them a competitive edge you may not be able to predict or overcome. It goes back to the old childhood warning: if you play with matches, you're going to get burned.

Feeling angry after being duped by a sociopath is normal (been there, done that). The more you understand about what just happened and how to protect yourself in the future, however, the better you will feel. Remember, stooping to their level is unlikely to end well. Creating more chaos and turmoil does not lessen your pain. Engaging in battle with a sociopath is like stepping on a bug that squirts you with slime. Your shoes deserve better. As Martha Stout points out, "Living well is the best revenge."

Don't Take It Personally: It's Not You - It's Them

Many empathetic people, myself included, beat themselves up for being gullible enough to be duped by a sociopath. As people with empathy, we try to project that empathy on the sociopath and attempt to understand how the sociopath could have treated us so badly. We forget the fundamental fact—sociopaths are not like us. It is not personal that they betrayed us. They are simply playing their self-concocted games, and using us was a way to alleviate their boredom. We didn't do anything wrong. It isn't personal—it's sociopathic.

You are not alone. After being a sociopath's target, you may feel foolish and stupid for falling for the lies and deception. You may blame yourself and feel ashamed, thinking you shouldn't tell anyone about what happened. Keeping it hidden inside will only make the hurt linger longer. I have been amazed at how many people have been burned by sociopaths. Everybody knows one. Talk to your family and friends. Strongly consider seeking out professional support. Suffering alone helps no one and delays your ability to learn from your mistakes and move on with your life.

Interactions with sociopaths may leave you wondering whom you can trust. I am a very trusting person. It's simply how I am made. It has served me well as a hospice geriatrician where I must prescribe pain medications to patients at the end of life. Other doctors fear being fooled by drug-seeking patients lying about their pain, and this fear prevents them from prescribing medication to some patients who truly are suffering. For me, I would rather be fooled sometimes rather than find out later that patients endured pain because I didn't believe them. Even terminally ill drug addicts deserve a peaceful death. There have been times when I discovered that I had been conned and pain medications were being diverted. My trust was violated, and I did not offer any second chances. Those patients were discharged from hospice, and their drug supply was cut off. I trust people until they show me they cannot be trusted—then I'm done. The same goes for social interactions. I offer a certain amount of trust to anyone I meet— but since my experience with a sociopath, I maintain boundaries as well. It is not an either/or situation. You can be kind to strangers while maintaining boundaries. No one has access to my heart, my family, or my pocketbook without earning my deeper trust over time through focused observation and investigation. Trustworthy people will have patience while they earn your trust.

Remember that sociopaths often target those with the most love to give. They instinctively hurt the most empathetic because they envy what they do not have. Empathy is a strength. It enables you to experience some of the most treasured human experiences possible including love and compassion. Don't feel bad about having empathy and experiencing deep emotions. It may be painful sometimes, but it is so much better than being empty inside. Even when you are unjustly hurt, it is not your fault—no one deserves to be abused.

I don't understand how someone could treat me this way!

DON'T TAKE IT PERSONALLY

Learn More - It Could Save Your Life

Just when you think that you know everything about sociopathy, you realize that no one does. Don't' let your understanding of the sociopath be static. Be open to new understandings of them now and in the future for this is an evolving field, and there is always more to learn.

Again, like so many things when it comes to human behavior, the recommendations here will slightly change based on how you like to operate and the type of person you consider yourself to be. If all of this seems to be too much for you, if you prefer to be accepting of everyone and refuse to believe that not everyone is like you, that some people are just "different"— do so at your own peril. There's nothing that will make a sociopath lick their lips more than an unsuspecting victim who repeatedly is giving their questionable behavior the benefit of the doubt. It's one thing to be open minded—it's another to leave yourself vulnerable to attack. Just as a gazelle on the savannah might not want to walk over to a lion's den to befriend them, an empathetic person needs to be attentive to the danger that lurks when a sociopath draws near. Without an awareness of the possible traits and a system for protecting oneself, an empathetic person is no better than an oblivious gazelle munching on the grass with their eyes closed while a lion readies itself to pounce.

LEARN MORE

Knowledge is power

The Bigger Picture - Growing Bigger Every Day

Since the majority of you reading this are not sociopaths or sexopaths, it's unlikely you will find much joy in "beating" them at their game. The thrill of winning doesn't drive you as it drives them. To that end, you would do well to remember that the game you are part of (if you want to call it that) is part of a much, much bigger picture: that of the human experience at large and the global good. The seemingly tiny behavior choices ultimately accelerate or slow down the sociopathic onslaught taking place around the world.

In all of this, remember the larger issue—which isn't who around you happens to be a sociopath or sexopath, but how you might protect yourself and greater society from falling victim to sociopathic behavior. While sociopaths are focused on winning their games of personal gain and satisfaction, it's up to you to keep the greater good in mind. Being open minded is one thing, but in the case of sociopathy, it might get you—and indeed the whole of society—raped or killed. #MeToo is the symptom. Sexopathy is the cause. Pathological lying and dreams of domination by world leaders can be sure signs of a sociopath—and our entire existence can be hanging in a perilous state based on sociopathic whims.

We're so open minded, our brains fell out!

Conclusion

You know a sociopath—a type of person who is not like the rest of us who lacks empathy and a conscience. Sociopaths view the world as a game, and you and I are pawns to be manipulated for their personal gain. Using their deceptive charm and pathological lies, sociopaths control our world in business, government, entertainment, and even religion. At least 1 in 25 people fall on The Sociopath Spectrum meaning most of us interact with one every day, yet few of us recognize our danger. After all, you can't see what you are not looking for. With the help of The Sexopath Spotting Tool, however, awareness of sociopathic and sexopathic traits will be easier. But what comes after recognition? My empathetic soul cannot condone sending all sociopaths to jail or, as in earlier times, burning them at the stake. They are people—they are simply different from us.

Sociopaths see their altered brain function as an advantage—having no conscience or empathy means they have no problem lying and cheating to get what they want from the rest of us. As strange as it sounds, however, I pity them. Because of their inability to connect with other human beings on a soul level, they are incapable of experiencing love like the rest of us. I am not saying that sociopaths are not able to feel some kinds of love; but they are not able to experience

YOU KNOW

A SOCIOPATH

AT LEAST

1 IN 25

PEOPLE

the soul-connecting, empathetic love described in poetry, paintings, and literature throughout the ages—something that is seen as an idealistic goal for most of us. Sociopaths cannot love their families on a soul level either. Family members are more like possessions they defend out of ownership rather than because of the emotional exchange the rest of us feel for our loved ones. Love is one of the best things about being alive, and sociopaths will never experience it. Of course, most sociopaths do not realize that they do not love like the rest of us. How could they? They have never felt love and simply cannot imagine what they are missing. It is similar to trying to explain the color blue to someone blind since birth.

SOCIOPATHS NEVER EXPERIENCE EMPATHETIC LOVE

I pity the sociopaths incapable of empathetic love, but I am writing this book for the empathetic majority. Since I'm empathetic, I worry that other empathetic people are getting fooled and abused like I was. The empathetic majority is not playing by the same rules as the sociopaths, because we are not even aware that we are playing their convoluted, dangerous games. We think taking care of our families, participating in the local community, going to work, and hoping for prosperity is what life is all about. We have had no idea that we are also pawns in the sociopaths' game. I feel things deeply, and I truly believe that empathetic people of the world will be better off if they are aware of sociopaths and learn to recognize them. In this age of the "all-inclusive" and "embrace everyone" mentality, we are forgetting to look at the reality of the situation. We are different from one another. We cannot come together until we recognize and accept our differences.

TIME'S UP

Perhaps the next step after recognition involves accountability and transparency. When did lying become so acceptable and even expected? Often empathetic people are silent in an effort to be polite. We overlook inconsistencies we see in possible sociopaths and sexopaths because we do not want to make a scene. Perhaps the time has come to follow the drive of the #MeToo movement and no longer be afraid to speak out. Anyone can act sociopathically or sexopathically in the wrong circumstances, but now we must investigate the intent behind the actions. Time is officially up.

When you see sociopathic behavior, don't let it slide. If you do not want to call someone out for a blatant lie, at least go talk to someone else about it. Begin to question, observe, and discuss. We can only be pitted against each other if we allow sociopaths free rein. Their lies only work if we don't communicate with one another. Our greatest strength is each other. Communication is the key to creating a better tomorrow.

Avoidance is the best strategy in dealing with a sociopath. It isn't always possible, but is the safest for your well-being. Stay off their radar. If you work for a sociopath, consider changing jobs. If you love someone and suspect that he or she is a sociopath or sexopath, then at least temper your love with this new knowledge and awareness. In reality, detecting a sociopath or sexopath is not nearly as important as simply distancing yourself from someone who may be one. When it comes to people you

AVOIDANCE

KEEP YOUR FAMILY SAFE

suspect of being sociopaths, you need to be so far removed from their influence that whether or not they fall on this spectrum no longer affects you. Making a diagnosis is not what is important. Staying safe is what matters, because by the time you are 99% sure that you are dealing with a sociopath, you will have already been hurt. At the end of the day, when all the philosophies and ideas can be evaluated, we are left to take care of our friends and families in the best manner possible. We cannot risk their well-being by engaging in the fruitless hope of sociopaths growing a conscience.

If you find yourself feeling more afraid than ever with this new awareness and more suspicious of every new acquaintance, then I invite you to turn this around and see it in the exact opposite light. With this new knowledge, you can be more confident in understanding the actions and thought processes of people you know and meet. You didn't know about sociopaths before, but now you will have the ability to recognize potential dangers. It isn't necessary that you understand the subject totally. No one does. You simply need to comprehend the basics and trust in the good that this knowledge will bring you.

Most people do not understand what sociopaths are. They have heard the word before, but its exact meaning is still fuzzy. After reading this book, you are in the minority of the empathetic majority who realize there are people without conscience or the ability to feel empathy. Ideally, in the future everybody will understand sociopaths exist. Everyone will insist that jobs requiring truthfulness and empathy are simply not a good fit for the sociopaths of the world. Until everyone is aware of the problem, it would help if you spread the word. Give someone this book—or, better yet, buy more books and hand them out as gifts! My empathetic soul already feels guilty for the self-serving nature of that last sentence, but, in all seriousness, you know someone who has suffered at the hands of a person *pretending* to have a conscience. They may blame themselves, but it isn't their fault. This book will speed their recovery process as they become aware of the predators among us. Please, pass this information on. You can change the world for the better by helping people understand sociopathy.

We have a very harsh opinion of ourselves and our state of humanity. The empathetic majority is actually much more loving, kind, and moral than we give ourselves credit for. We've been judging ourselves for what is really the effect of allowing sociopaths too much power, control, and influence in our society. The dangerous fallacies we have all been taught about human nature are really the truth about sociopaths. Most humans are not warlike. We want peace. We want our families to laugh and know that tomorrow will be a good day. The sociopaths want war. They feed off the malignant energy and the chaos. If the empathetic majority can come to see how good we all are—outside of the few who are lacking in empathy and conscience—the world will become a better place for everyone. We need to rethink who we are as humans, excluding the minority of us who are sociopaths.

Imagine what our world would look like if the empathetic majority were in charge. It would seem like a utopia compared to what we know now. Every little part of our reality would be improved and less painful. Our innate desire to help one another would be our defining moment of victory. It is through kindness that we will change the world. How revolutionary it would be when we simply stop giving sociopaths our trust and our loyalty. Surely a new day will dawn when we shine the light of truth upon them.

A NEW DAWN
OF TRUTH

EMPATHS
UNITE

<u>Glossary</u>

Amygdala - The part of the brain that is responsible for emotions, survival instincts, and memory. It is a hub through which signals pass to the next area of the brain for processing.

Anti-Social Personality Disorder (ASPD) - Currently the diagnosis in the DSM-V that is meant to represent sociopaths and psychopaths. Many researchers feel it is too broad with too high a focus on criminality. Approximately 75% of prisoners are ASPD but only 15-25% of prisoners are true psychopaths.

Conscience - The inner feeling or voice that acts as a guide to the rightness or wrongness of our behavior that urges us to do right.

Conscious - Awake, not unconscious, asleep, or in a coma.

Devalue - *please see Sexopath Love Cycle.*

Diagnostic Statistical Manual of Mental Disorders (DSM-V) - Published by the American Psychiatric Association, the DSM is essentially the "Diagnostic Bible" for any medical professional dealing with mental health and is considered the standard classification for mental disorders.

Discard - *please see Sexopath Love Cycle.*

Edutainment - A literary genre that combines education and entertainment utilizing humerous drawings and fictional characters to explain a relevant topic. It is entertaining education.

Empathetic Majority - most people who have a conscience and the ability to feel empathy.

Empathy - The ability to feel and understand what another person is feeling.

Functional Magnetic Resonance Imaging (fMRI) - A high resolution imaging technique used to measure brain activity by detecting changes associated with blood flow.

Frontal lobe - The part of the brain involved in such activities as motor function, problem solving, spontaneity, memory, language, initiation, judgement, impulse control, and social and sexual behavior.

Gaslighting - The use of psychological means to manipulate someone into questioning his or her sanity, memory, and perception.

Hippocampus - The region of the brain that regulates emotions and is associated with memory, particularly long-term memory.

Hypersexuality - Compulsive sexual behavior, also identified as sexual addiction. It is marked by excessive preoccupation with sexual fantasies, urges, or behavior to the degree it negatively effects the individual's life.

Id - The pleasure seeking part of the mind as revealed by Sigmund Freud that ignores any possible consequences of a decision or action and focuses on the possible pleasure that can come from a behavior.

Idealize - *please see Sexopath Love Cycle.*

Love Bombing - An overwhelming attempt to secure someone's attentions and affection generally through flattering comments, gifts, and love notes.

#MeToo - A movement primarily composed of women (although more men are starting to speak up) objecting to sexual harassment and abuse in the work place while seeking suitable punishment for sexual predators.

Micro-inflections - Subtle physical signs in the facial expressions that show the true feelings of an individual. For empathetic people this includes such emotions as compassion and concern. For sociopaths, the inflections may illustrate extreme anger and frustration. They are often very fleeting and may not be picked up on a conscious level.

Mirror Neurons - Neurons that fire when someone observes the same action performed by someone else that has previously been experienced. Seeing someone's fingers crushed in a car door results in a firing some of the same neurons in the observer as the person with hurt fingers.

Mnemonic - A device such as a pattern of letters, ideas, or associations that assists in memory retention.

Narcissim - An excessive interest in oneself and one's physical appearance, illustrated by extreme selfishness and a grandiose view of one's talents and abilities. Usually accompanied by an craving for admiration. All sociopaths are narcissists but not all narcissists are sociopaths.

NashvilleKitty - the ultimate anti-hero sexopath in *69 Shades of Nashville: Sociopathic Sex Southern Style* by Nicole Kelly, M.D. Although fictionalized to a point where she is unidentifiable, she was inspired by a real life sexopath who embezzeled over $700,000 from Dr. Kelly's medical practice. What started as a nightmare, turned into the perfect character study to educate the world about sexopaths.

Neurotypical - A phrase often used in the Autistic community to describe people with more typical thought processes. It is used by NashvilleKitty to identify a person who is not a sociopath—which is a negative term in her opinion.

Positron Emission Tomography (PET) Scan - A nuclear medicine imaging technique that can observe metabolic processes in the body. It shows which parts of the brain are being used during activities or thoughts.

Predatory Stare - An intense, penetrating gazing of the eyes similar to the stare used by predators in the wild as they stalk their prey. In humans, it has sometimes been described as undressing someone with their eyes.

Psychopath - A person without a conscience or empathy at the far end of the sociopathic/psychopathic spectrum scoring a 30 or greater out of 40 on the Psychopathy Checklist - Revised (PCL-R).

Psychopath-lite - A term used by Dr. James Fallon to describe those with psychopathic traits who do not make the cut off of 30 to reach the diagnosis of psychopath. The term "sociopath" is used in this book.

Psychopathy Checklist (PCL-R) - Created by Robert D. Hare, Ph.D., the checklist uses extensive interviews and collateral information to diagnose psychopaths. It was revised so now has an "R" added to it.

Sex Addiction - A range of excessive sexual behaviors that negatively affect the individual's life and, in many ways, is similar to other types of addiction including drug, alcohol, and gambling.

Sexopath - A sociopath or psychopath with a sex addiction.

Sexopathic Behavior - When an empathetic person or a sociopath/ psychopath acts in a sexually deviant manner or has sex without empathy.

Sexopath Love Cycle - There are three stages in the love cycle: 1. Idealize (often with love bombing), 2. Devalue (hot/cold, sweet then incredibly cruel and can include gaslighting), 3. Discard (ending the relationship often in a very cruel and abrupt manner).

Sexopath Spotting Tool - A screening tool designed to help identify certain character traits in a person that may spell out a pattern of sexopathic, sociopathic, or psychopathic behavior featuring a 20-letter mnemonic called GLIMPSE BEHIND THE MASK. It describes specific traits that can help empathetic people be aware of potential danger.

69 Shades of Nashville: Sociopathic Sex Southern Style - A novel by Nicole Kelly, M.D. that explores the sexual adventures of a female sexopath who joins a cheaters' website and was inspired by an actual nurse. It takes you inside the mind of a sexopath so you can truly understand how these people think.

Sociopath - A person without a conscience or empathy who, if tested on the PCL-R, would score at least a 15 but does not make the cut off of 30 to be a full-blown psychopath. This is the definition used in this book. Researchers debate on the usefulness of this word, but I think it helps to make this subject more understandable.

Super Ego - Representative of ideals, it considers the consequences of behavior, breaking down actions and thoughts into right and wrong through a moral compass. Sigmund Freud initiated the concept of the Super Ego.

The Pleasure Center - Dopamine release in the brain is so tied with the sensation of pleasure that this region is known as the brain's pleasure center. All drugs of abuse, such as nicotine and heroin, cause a particularly powerful surge of dopamine to this area.

The Sociopath Spectrum - A spectrum to describe the sociopathic/ psychopathic spectrum that ranges from sociopath to psychopath with different levels along the scale.

Time's Up - Originated primarily by actors who had suffered sexual harrassment in the entertainment industry, this movement has pressed for the elimination of the Hollywood casting couch and sexual mistreatment across all areas.

Warrior Gene - Most often found in men, the individuals who inherit this gene tend to have decreased fear of harm or death combined with higher levels of aggression.

__Additional Resources__

After thousands of hours of research reading books, articles, websites, and multiple other sources, the following short list includes many of the best resources to enable you to delve deeper into this topic. There is so much out there, but this will give you a place to start to learn more about this fascinating topic. I have added comments about the selections so you can decide what will be the most useful for you and your situation.

Babiak, Paul and Hare, Robert D., *Snakes in Suits: When Psychopaths Go to Work*, New York: Harper Collins, 2006. An excellent resource about people on The Sociopath Spectrum in the work place. Highly recommend.

Birch, Adelyn, website *www.psychopathsandlove.com*. Useful website for those leaving an abusive relationship with a predator.

Ciaramicoli, Arthur and Ketcham, Katherine, *The Power of Empathy: A Practical Guide to Creating Intimacy, Self-Understanding, and Lasting Love,* New York: Dutton, 1997. Even though over 20 years old, this book on empathy never goes out of style. Empathy is powerful, and by embracing it we will have a better tomorrow.

Cleckley, Hervey, *The Mask of Sanity: An Attempt to Clarify Some Issues About the So-Called Psychopathic Personality,* Brattleboro: Echo Point Books & Media, First edition 1941, Last edition 1976. The first modern book on this subject that still remains valuable to this day.

Dutton, Kevin, *The Wisdom of Psychopaths: What Saints, Spies, and Serial Killers Can Teach Us About Success,* New York: Scientific American, 2012. This book takes a rather different approach to this subject as the author's father and one of his best friends are psychopaths, and he suggests that just the right amount of psychopathy could be advantageous. He even undergoes an experiement during which his mind is made "psychopathic" for around 20 minutes where he has adulterous thoughts and decreased fear while feeling invincible. It definitely made me think, although I'm not sure I agree with his conclusion.

Fallon, James, *The Psychopath Inside: A Neuroscientist's Personal Journey into the Dark Side of the Brain,* New York: Penguin Group, 2013. A captivating tale of a neuro-researcher who found (completely by accident) that his brain scan looked psychopathic. Dr. Fallon was kind enough to allow me to interview him and has a unique perspective regarding the psychopathic mind. Highly recommend.

Hare, Robert D., *Without Conscience: The Disturbing World of the Psychopaths Among Us,* New York: Pocket Books, 1993. This is a classic by the pioneer of this field in the second half of the 20th century. His stories and explanations paint the picture of this devious personality type. Excellent book.

Haycock, Dean, *Murderous Minds: Exploring the Criminal Psychopathic Brain: Neurological Imaging and the Manifestation of Evil,* New York: Pegasus Books, 2014. This probably has too much neuroscience for the general reader, but I do recommend it for those who want to examine the brain in depth.

Kelly, Nicole, *69 Shades of Nashville: Sociopathic Sex Southern Style,* Nashville: JACC Publishing, 2018. Ok, I'm plugging my own book—but I do think it will further your understanding of the sexopathic mind. This is truly how sexopaths think and understanding how they think will help you protect yourself from manipulation and abuse. It also has laugh-out-loud drawings and jokes that will make this one of the most entertaining educational books of all time. Check out the audio book for the craziest read-along ever!

Kiehl, Kent, *The Psychopath Whisperer: The Science of Those Without Conscience,* New York: Crown Pulishers, 2014. Although this is probably a bit too technical for the general reader, I found it to be a very interesting book by the man with an fMRI machine in a big truck that he takes from prison to prison studying psychopaths.

MacKenzie, Jackson, *Psychopath Free: Recovering from Emotionally Abusive Relationships with Narcissists, Sociopaths, and Other Toxic People,* New York: Berkley Books, 2015. Extremely helpful book written for the general public as well as a useful website *www.psychopathfree.com* for anyone coming out of an abusive relationship. Highly recommend.

Navarro, Joe. *Dangerous Personalities: An FBI Profiler Shows You How to Identify and Protect Yourself from Harmful People,* New York: Rodale, 2014. Joe Navarro is a retired FBI special agent whose book explores several different types of "dangerous personalities" including predators. His style is easy to understand and quite informative.

Reid, Meloy, *The Psychopathic Mind: Origins, Dynamics, and Treatment,* Lanham: Rowman & Littlefield Publishers, 2004. Although Dr. Meloy claims his book is a good sedative, it offers useful information regarding this personality type. Dr. Meloy's empathy was apparent during my PCL-R training as he went above and beyond to increase understanding of how to diagnosis a psychopath.

Salter, Anna, *Predators: Pedophiles, Rapists, and Other Sex Offenders: Who They Are, How They Operate, and How We Can Protect Ourselves and Our Children,* New York: Basic Books, 2003. This book literally gave me nightmares. The chapter on sadists began with a warning, but I figured, "I'm a medical professional—I can handle it." All I can say is—it's deeply disturbing. However, it did enable an Aha moment for me as she explored how these people who are so different from most of us truly think. This book changed me.

Samenow, Stanton. *Before It's Too Late: Why Some Kids Get Into Trouble—and What Parents Can Do About It,* New York: Times Books, 1998. This book is already 20 years old, but it is a MUST read for any parent with a child expressing sociopathic traits. This book may change the outcome of a budding sociopathic/psychopathic child from prison to functional adult. Getting professional help from an expert in this field is also an urgent necessity and the sooner the better. Strongly recommend.

Schouten, Ronald and Silver, James, *Almost a Psychopath: Do I (or Does Someone I Know) Have a Problem with Manipulation and Lack of Empathy?,* Center City: Hazelden, 2012. Although I disagree with some of the advice given in this book (such as confronting someone without a conscience about their lack of empathy—could be dangerous in the wrong circumstances), it is well written with interesting examples and could be helpful as you further explore this topic.

Simon, George, *In Sheep's Clothing: Understanding and Dealing with Manipulative People,* Little Rock: Parkhust Brothers, 1996 and 2010. Well written and very informative for the empathetic majority. Highly recommend.

Stout, Martha, *The Sociopath Next Door: 1 in 25 Ordinary Americans Secretly Has No Conscience and Can Do Anything at All Without Feeling Guilty. Who is the Devil* <u>You</u> *Know,* New York: Harmony Books, 2005. A captivating book that really helps in understanding this personality type from the inside out. It is one of the best books out there in explaining this often confusing topic. Highly recommend.

Thomas, M.E., *Confessions of a Sociopath: A Life Spent Hiding in Plain Sight,* New York: Crown Publishing Group, 2013. I discovered this book right after I finished writing *69 Shades of Nashville* and nearly fell out of my seat when she said "dear reader" (a common phrase used by my fictional NashvilleKitty). The similarities were almost eerie. This book offers an intriguing glimpse inside the mind of a sociopath and promotes the understanding that being a sociopath does not make someone evil—although being sociopathic may predispose someone to do evil things. Doing evil is a choice. M.E. Thomas is a member of the Mormon Church and by following religious guidelines, she is a productive member of society. She has a fascinating website *www.SociopathWorld.com* where sociopaths and empaths hash it out over diverse subjects. Definitely worth a look.

Transcendence, *Master Dealing with Psychopaths, Sociopaths, Narcissists—A Handbook for the Empath—Kindle Edition Version 3.0,* 2017. Written in everyday language without scientific terminology with very useful advice for the empathetic majority. Highly recommend.

69 Shades of Nashville: Sociopathic Sex Southern Style

NashvilleKitty is a sociopath. Don't worry. She doesn't want to hurt you. She just wants to screw you, literally. After years doing it the old-fashioned way, NashvilleKitty joins a cheaters' dating website sending her on the scintillating, full-throttle, erotic thrill-ride of her dreams. The serial tryst artist is keenly aware of her sociopathic powers, leveraging them to get anything—and anyone—she wants. The more men (and occasional women) she possesses, the more she craves, until she finds a soul as pure as they come among adulterers. As danger and violence threaten to turn her sweet cheater's dream into a nightmare, this special someone shows her a way out. But can this sociopath change?

About The Author

Nicole Kelly, M.D. is the nom de plume of an established Nashville physician who had first hand experience dealing with the manipulations of a sociopath who also turned out to be a sociopathic sex addict or sexopath. Her award-winning first novel *69 Shades of Nashville: Sociopathic Sex Southern Style* explores the adulterous adventures of NashvilleKitty on a cheaters' dating site resulting in murder and suspense. Although fictionalized for legal reasons, the novel is narrated by an actual sexopath inspired by a true story. You are transported inside the mind of a sociopathic sex addict—if we can understand how they think, we can beat them at their own game.

Her first non-fiction work *Charming Cheaters: Protect Yourself from the Sociopaths, Psychopaths, and Sexopaths in Your Life* reveals the predators among us, hiding in plain sight. Written from her home in Nashville, Tennessee, Nicole Kelly, M.D. aims to educate in an entertaining format and has included many drawings to give a visual explanation of the written text. Education does not have to be boring, and the sooner the empathetic majority learn to recognize sociopaths, psychopaths, and sexopaths—the safer we will be. Visit NicoleKellyMD.com for free downloads including the opportunity to delve deeper into the nature of the sexopathic mind next door.

9 780999 186152